Heart Healthy Cookbook for Beginners:

1800 Days of Simple, Low-Fat, Low-Sodium Recipes. Expert Tips for Complete Guide to Lifelong Wellness & Bonus

Abilene Higgs

Table of Content

Welcome Message

Introduction to the book and its purpose

Welcome to your empowering journey towards better heart health! This cookbook is designed with your unique needs in mind, whether you are taking the first steps in improving your cardiovascular health or looking to deepen your understanding of heart-healthy living. Our goal is to provide you with the knowledge, tools, and delicious recipes that will help you embrace a lifestyle that supports and enhances your heart health.

This book's purpose is not only to offer a collection of recipes but also to educate and inspire. We understand that heart health is a critical component of overall wellness, and making informed choices about what you eat can significantly impact your cardiovascular system. This book, written in clear and accessible language, aims to demystify the concept of heart-healthy eating, making it easy and enjoyable for everyone to understand and apply.

Heart disease remains one of the leading causes of mortality worldwide, and many of its risk factors are related to diet and lifestyle. By choosing to focus on heart health, you are taking a proactive step towards a healthier, longer life. This book is here to guide and support you on that journey, offering evidence-based information and practical advice that you can incorporate into your daily routine.

Our approach is holistic, considering not only the nutritional content of your meals but also how to make heart-healthy cooking a sustainable and pleasurable part of your life. We've included chapters on essential ingredients and kitchen tools to make your cooking experience more efficient and enjoyable. Additionally, we cover basic cooking techniques that will help you confidently prepare low-fat and low-sodium meals, even if you are new to the kitchen.

The recipes in this book are crafted to be both delicious and nutritious, proving that healthy eating does not mean sacrificing flavor. From quick and easy breakfasts to hearty dinners and guilt-free desserts, you'll find a variety of meals that cater to different tastes and preferences, whether you prefer [vegetarian, Mediterranean, or Asian-inspired dishes]. We've also included a chapter dedicated to snacks and appetizers, ensuring that you have heart-healthy options for every occasion.

But this book goes beyond just recipes. It includes comprehensive expert tips on nutrition, exercise, and lifestyle changes that are crucial for maintaining optimal heart health. You'll learn about the importance of balanced nutrition, ways to reduce sodium and fat intake, and the benefits of regular physical activity. We also offer strategies for stress management and tips for building healthy habits that you can sustain in the long term.

To help you get started, we've included a bonus 30-day meal plan with weekly planners and shopping lists. This plan is designed to simplify your meal preparation, ensure that you are consistently making heart-healthy choices, and kickstart your journey to better heart health. Each meal is thoughtfully planned to provide balanced nutrition and delightful flavors, making your journey to heart health both manageable and enjoyable.

In the appendices, you'll find a glossary of heart-healthy terms, which will help you understand the nutritional aspects of the recipes, conversion charts to make it easier to follow the recipes, and a list of resources for further reading, so you can continue to expand your knowledge on heart-healthy living. These sections are designed to support your learning and provide you with additional tools to succeed in your heart-healthy journey.

We hope that this book will be a valuable resource for you, offering not just recipes, but also the inspiration and knowledge needed to make heart-healthy living a natural and enjoyable part of your life. It's time to take the first step towards a healthier heart and a happier you! Let's get started!

The importance of heart health

Heart health is a cornerstone of overall well-being, impacting every aspect of our lives. The heart, a marvel of biological engineering, pumps blood throughout our bodies, delivering oxygen and essential nutrients to tissues and organs while removing waste products. Maintaining a healthy heart is crucial for sustaining this vital process and ensuring we live long, active, and fulfilling lives.

The importance of heart health cannot be overstated. Cardiovascular disease, which includes heart disease and stroke, is a leading cause of death globally. Many of these conditions are preventable through lifestyle changes, particularly those related to diet and exercise. By focusing on heart health, we can significantly reduce the risk of developing these diseases, enhancing both the quality and longevity of our lives.

A heart-healthy lifestyle is about more than just preventing disease; it's about thriving. When our hearts are healthy, we have more energy, better stamina, and improved mental clarity. We can engage more fully in the activities we love, from playing with our children or grandchildren to pursuing our favorite hobbies. A healthy heart supports a vibrant, active life, enabling us to make the most of every day.

Diet plays a pivotal role in heart health. The foods we choose can either contribute to heart disease or help prevent it. For instance, diets high in saturated fats, trans fats, sodium, and added sugars are linked to an increased risk of heart disease. On the other hand, diets rich in fruits like [apples and oranges], vegetables like [broccoli and spinach], whole grains like [oats and quinoa], lean proteins like [chicken and fish], and healthy fats like [avocado and olive oil] can lower the risk. By making conscious choices about what we eat, we can directly influence our heart health and overall well-being.

Regular physical activity is another essential component of heart health. Exercise strengthens the heart muscle, improves blood circulation, and helps maintain a healthy weight. It also reduces stress, lowers blood pressure, and increases HDL (good) cholesterol levels. But it's not just about the physical benefits. Exercise also boosts our mood, improves our mental clarity, and enhances our overall well-being. Even moderate exercise, like brisk walking or cycling, can have significant benefits for heart health, leaving us feeling energized and uplifted.

In addition to diet and exercise, managing stress is crucial for maintaining heart health. Chronic stress can lead to behaviors and factors that increase heart disease risk, such as high blood pressure, smoking, or overeating. Taking time for self-care and learning stress management techniques, such as mindfulness, meditation, or yoga, can help mitigate these risks and promote a sense of calm and well-being. Remember, your well-being is important and should be a priority in your heart health journey.

Smoking cessation is also vital for heart health. Smoking damages the lining of the arteries increases blood pressure and reduces the amount of oxygen that reaches the body's tissues. Quitting smoking is one of the best things you can do for your heart, significantly reducing the risk of heart disease and improving overall health.

Monitoring and managing health metrics, such as blood pressure, cholesterol levels, and blood sugar, is essential for preventing heart disease. Regular check-ups with healthcare providers, where they can measure these metrics and provide guidance on maintaining them at healthy levels, can help detect early signs of heart problems and allow for timely intervention. Staying informed about your heart health empowers you to make proactive choices and adjustments as needed.

The journey to heart health is a lifelong commitment but yields tremendous rewards. By prioritizing heart health, we reduce the risk of disease and enhance our ability to enjoy life to its fullest. This book is designed to be your companion on this journey, offering practical advice, delicious recipes, and expert tips to help you make heart-healthy living a natural and enjoyable part of your life.

Remember, every positive change, no matter how small, contributes to a healthier heart and a better quality of life. Embrace this journey with optimism and dedication, and take pride in your steps towards a healthier, happier you. Here's to your heart health and a future filled with vitality and well-being.

Heart Health Understanding

Basic anatomy and function of the heart

The heart is not just an organ, it's the central pillar of our circulatory system, essential for our survival. Understanding its basic anatomy and function is not just crucial, it's a necessity for appreciating the importance of heart health and making informed decisions about our lifestyle and diet.

Anatomically, the heart is a muscular organ about the size of a fist, located slightly to the left of the center of the chest. It comprises four chambers: two upper chambers called atria (singular: atrium) and two lower chambers called ventricles. The atria receive blood from the heart, while the ventricles pump blood from the heart.

The right side of the heart receives deoxygenated blood from the body and pumps it to the lungs for oxygenation. Specifically, blood enters the right atrium from the superior and inferior vena cavae and then flows into the right ventricle. When the proper ventricle contracts, it sends blood to the lungs via the pulmonary arteries.

The left side of the heart handles oxygenated blood from the lungs, pumping it to the rest of the body. Blood enters the left atrium from the pulmonary veins, moves into the left ventricle, and is pumped through the aorta to supply the body's tissues and organs with oxygen and nutrients.

Valves within the heart ensure the unidirectional blood flow, preventing backflow and maintaining efficient circulation. The tricuspid valve is between the right atrium and right ventricle, and the pulmonary valve is between the right ventricle and the pulmonary artery. On the left side, the mitral valve lies between the left atrium and left ventricle, while the aortic valve is between the left ventricle and the aorta. These valves open and close with each heartbeat, regulating blood flow and ensuring blood moves smoothly through the heart's chambers and into the arteries.

The heart's function is driven by an intricate electrical conduction system, which coordinates the heartbeat. The sinoatrial (SA) node, a small cluster of cells located in the right atrium, acts as the natural pacemaker, generating electrical impulses that spread through the atria, causing them to contract and push blood into the ventricles. These impulses then travel to the atrioventricular (AV) node, a group of cells located between the atria and ventricles, which delays the signal slightly before sending it down the bundle of His, a collection of specialized cells, and into the Purkinje fibers, a network of specialized muscle fibers. This system ensures that the ventricles contract in a coordinated manner, effectively pumping blood out of the heart.

The heart's muscular walls, known as the myocardium, are especially thick in the ventricles, providing the necessary force to pump blood throughout the body. The coronary arteries, which are located on the surface of the heart and supply the myocardium with oxygen-rich blood, are essential for its constant, vigorous activity. These arteries, like the branches of a tree, spread across the heart, ensuring that every part of the myocardium receives the oxygen and nutrients it needs to function optimally.

Understanding this basic anatomy and function reveals the heart's remarkable resilience and the critical importance of maintaining its health. The heart tirelessly beats around 100,000 times a day, pumping about 5 liters of blood per minute. This relentless activity underscores the need to support heart health through a balanced diet, regular exercise, and other heart-healthy practices.

By actively maintaining a healthy heart, we ensure that this vital organ can continue to perform its essential functions, supplying oxygen and nutrients to our bodies and enabling us to lead active, healthy lives. The subsequent chapters in this book will provide practical guidance on how to support your heart through nutritious recipes, lifestyle changes, and informed choices, empowering you to take control of your cardiovascular health.

Benefits of a heart-healthy diet

A heart-healthy diet is one of the most powerful tools we have for protecting and improving cardiovascular health. The foods we eat play a critical role in determining the health of our heart and blood vessels, impacting factors such as cholesterol levels, blood pressure, inflammation, and body weight. Embracing a diet that supports heart health can lead to numerous benefits, enhancing both quality and longevity of life.

1. Reduced Risk of Heart Disease: One of the primary benefits of a heart-healthy diet is a significantly reduced risk of developing heart disease. Diets rich in fruits, vegetables, whole grains, lean proteins, and healthy fats can lower levels of LDL (bad) cholesterol and triglycerides, which are key contributors to atherosclerosis—a condition where arteries become clogged with fatty deposits. This can prevent the formation of plaques that narrow arteries and lead to coronary artery disease and heart attacks.

2. Lower Blood Pressure: High blood pressure, or hypertension, is a major risk factor for heart disease and stroke. A heart-healthy diet emphasizes foods low in sodium and rich in potassium, magnesium, and calcium—nutrients that help regulate blood pressure. Consuming plenty of fruits, vegetables, and whole grains while limiting processed foods and added salts can help maintain healthy blood pressure levels.

3. Improved Cholesterol Levels: Healthy eating patterns can improve cholesterol levels by lowering LDL cholesterol and increasing HDL (good) cholesterol. Foods high in soluble fiber, such as oats, beans, and fruits, can help reduce LDL cholesterol levels by binding with cholesterol in the digestive system and removing it from the body. Healthy fats, such as those found in olive oil, avocados, and nuts, can increase HDL cholesterol, which helps remove LDL cholesterol from the bloodstream.

4. Weight Management: Maintaining a healthy weight is crucial for heart health, as obesity is a significant risk factor for heart disease. A heart-healthy diet focuses on nutrient-dense foods that provide essential vitamins and minerals without excessive calories. By choosing whole, unprocessed foods and balancing calorie intake with physical activity, you can achieve and maintain a healthy weight, reducing the strain on your heart and lowering your risk of developing heart-related conditions.

5. Reduced Inflammation: Chronic inflammation is a contributing factor to many heart diseases, including atherosclerosis and heart attacks. Anti-inflammatory foods, such as those rich in omega-3 fatty acids (found in fatty fish like salmon and flaxseeds), antioxidants (found in berries and leafy greens), and phytonutrients (found in a variety of colorful fruits and vegetables), can help reduce inflammation and protect the heart.

6. Better Blood Sugar Control: Managing blood sugar levels is important for heart health, particularly for individuals with diabetes or prediabetes. A heart-healthy diet includes complex carbohydrates with a low glycemic index, such as whole grains, legumes, and vegetables, which help maintain stable blood sugar levels. Avoiding refined sugars and processed carbohydrates can prevent spikes in blood sugar that contribute to insulin resistance and cardiovascular complications.

7. Enhanced Overall Health: A heart-healthy diet benefits more than just the heart. The same foods that support cardiovascular health also promote overall well-being. For example, fruits and vegetables are packed with vitamins, minerals, and fiber that support digestive health, boost the immune system, and improve skin health. Lean proteins, such as fish, poultry, and legumes, provide essential amino acids for muscle repair and maintenance. Healthy fats support brain function and reduce the risk of cognitive decline.

8. Improved Energy Levels: Eating a balanced diet with a variety of nutrient-rich foods can improve energy levels and reduce fatigue. Whole grains, lean proteins, and healthy fats provide sustained energy throughout the day, while avoiding energy crashes associated with high-sugar, high-fat diets. This increased energy supports an active lifestyle, which is also beneficial for heart health.

9. Mental Health Benefits: Nutrition plays a significant role in mental health, and a heart-healthy diet can improve mood and cognitive function. Foods rich in omega-3 fatty acids, antioxidants, and B vitamins have been shown to reduce symptoms of depression and anxiety. Maintaining a healthy diet can also enhance cognitive function, reducing the risk of conditions like dementia and Alzheimer's disease.

10. Longevity: Adopting a heart-healthy diet is associated with increased longevity. Studies have shown that people who follow diets rich in plant-based foods, lean proteins, and healthy fats tend to live longer and have a lower risk of chronic diseases. The Mediterranean diet, for example, is well-known for its benefits in promoting heart health and extending lifespan.

Practical Steps to Adopt a Heart-Healthy Diet:

- **Increase fruit and vegetable intake:** Aim for at least five servings of fruits and vegetables daily, focusing on a variety of colors to ensure a range of nutrients.

- **Choose whole grains:** Replace refined grains with whole grains like brown rice, quinoa, oats, and whole wheat products.
- **Include healthy fats:** Opt for sources of healthy fats, such as olive oil, nuts, seeds, and fatty fish, while limiting saturated and trans fats.
- **Select lean proteins:** Incorporate lean meats, poultry, fish, legumes, and plant-based proteins into your meals.
- **Limit sodium:** Reduce salt intake by choosing fresh foods over processed ones and using herbs and spices for flavor.
- **Control portion sizes:** Be mindful of portion sizes to avoid overeating, which can contribute to weight gain and heart strain.
- **Stay hydrated:** Drink plenty of water and limit sugary drinks and alcohol.

By embracing a heart-healthy diet, you are taking a proactive step towards protecting your heart and enhancing your overall health. The recipes and tips in this book are designed to make heart-healthy eating delicious, enjoyable, and sustainable, empowering you to live a vibrant and healthy life.

Getting Started with Heart-Healthy Cooking

List of must-have pantry items

Welcome to the essential heart-healthy ingredients section, where we'll stock your pantry with nutritious staples to support your cardiovascular health. Having these items on hand will make it easier to create delicious and nutritious meals that nourish your heart and body. Here's a list of must-have pantry items:

1. Whole Grains:

Whole grains are rich in fiber, vitamins, and minerals, making them an excellent choice for heart health. Stock up on options like: Brown rice, Quinoa, Whole wheat pasta, Oats, Barley

2. Legumes:

Beans, lentils, and chickpeas are nutrient powerhouses, packed with fiber, protein, and antioxidants. They're versatile ingredients that can be used in soups, salads, stews, and more. Include: Black beans, Kidney beans, Lentils, Chickpeas (garbanzo beans), Split peas

3. Healthy Fats:

Incorporate sources of healthy fats into your pantry to support heart health.
These include: Olive oil (extra virgin), Avocado oil, Nuts (almonds, walnuts, pistachios) Seeds (chia seeds, flaxseeds), Nut butters (almond butter, peanut butter)

4. Canned Fish: Canned fish are convenient sources of omega-3 fatty acids, which are beneficial for heart health.
 Choose: Canned salmon, Canned tuna (preferably packed in water), Canned sardines

5. Herbs and Spices:

Add flavor to your dishes without relying on salt by stocking up on herbs and spices. Some heart-healthy options include: Garlic powder, Onion powder, Turmeric, Cinnamon, Basil, Oregano, Rosemary, Thyme

6. Low-Sodium Broth and Stocks: Broths and stocks are versatile bases for soups, stews, and sauces. Opt for low-sodium varieties to minimize your sodium intake.

7. Vinegars and Citrus Juices: Enhance the flavor of your dishes with vinegars and citrus juices. They add brightness without extra calories or sodium. Consider: Balsamic vinegar, , Apple cider vinegar Lemon juice, Lime juice

8. Dried Herbs and Spices: In addition to fresh herbs, keep a selection of dried herbs and spices on hand for added flavor and convenience. Examples include: Dried basil, Dried oregano, Dried thyme, Ground cumin, Ground paprika

9. Tomato Products: Tomato products are versatile ingredients that add depth of flavor to many dishes. Stock up on: Canned diced tomatoes, Tomato paste, Tomato sauce (look for no-added-salt varieties)

10. Whole Grain Flour: If you enjoy baking, consider using whole grain flours as alternatives to refined flours. Options include whole wheat flour, almond flour, and oat flour.

11. Non-Dairy Milk Alternatives: For those who prefer non-dairy options, keep shelf-stable non-dairy milks like almond milk, oat milk, or soy milk in your pantry.

By keeping these essential heart-healthy ingredients in your pantry, you'll be well-equipped to whip up nutritious meals that support your cardiovascular health. Experiment with different combinations and recipes to discover new favorites while nourishing your heart and body. Happy cooking!

Benefits of specific ingredients for heart health

In addition to stocking your pantry with essential heart-healthy ingredients, it's important to understand the specific benefits these ingredients offer for your cardiovascular health. Let's explore the key benefits of some of the ingredients commonly found in heart-healthy recipes:

1. Whole Grains: Whole grains like brown rice, quinoa, and oats are rich in fiber, which plays a crucial role in heart health. Fiber helps lower LDL (bad) cholesterol levels by binding to cholesterol in the digestive system and removing it from the body. Additionally, whole grains contain vitamins, minerals, and phytonutrients that support overall cardiovascular health and reduce the risk of heart disease.

2. Legumes: Beans, lentils, and chickpeas are excellent sources of plant-based protein and fiber. The soluble fiber found in legumes helps lower LDL cholesterol levels and regulate blood sugar levels, reducing the risk of heart disease and type 2 diabetes. Legumes are also low in fat and high in potassium, magnesium, and folate, which contribute to heart health by promoting healthy blood pressure levels and reducing inflammation.

3. Healthy Fats: Healthy fats, such as those found in olive oil, nuts, and seeds, are an essential component of a heart-healthy diet. These fats contain monounsaturated and polyunsaturated fats, which help lower LDL cholesterol levels and reduce inflammation in the body. Omega-3 fatty acids, found in fatty fish like salmon and in flaxseeds and walnuts, are particularly beneficial for heart health, as they can help lower triglyceride levels and reduce the risk of heart disease.

4. Fatty Fish: Fatty fish like salmon, mackerel, and sardines are rich in omega-3 fatty acids, which have been shown to have numerous benefits for heart health. Omega-3 fatty acids help reduce inflammation, lower triglyceride levels and prevent the formation of blood clots, reducing the risk of heart attack and stroke. Including fatty fish in your diet regularly can help support overall cardiovascular health.

5. Nuts and Seeds: Nuts and seeds are nutrient-dense foods that provide a variety of heart-healthy nutrients, including healthy fats, protein, fiber, vitamins, and minerals. They are particularly rich in monounsaturated and polyunsaturated fats, which help lower LDL cholesterol levels and reduce the risk of heart disease. Nuts and seeds also contain antioxidants and other bioactive compounds that have been shown to have protective effects on the heart.

6. Fruits and Vegetables: Fruits and vegetables are an essential part of a heart-healthy diet, as they are low in calories and high in vitamins, minerals, fiber, and antioxidants. Eating a variety of fruits and vegetables can help lower blood pressure, reduce inflammation, improve cholesterol levels, and protect against heart disease and stroke. Incorporating a colorful array of fruits and vegetables into your meals ensures that you're getting a wide range of heart-healthy nutrients.

By incorporating these specific ingredients into your diet regularly, you can reap the many benefits they offer for heart health. Whether you're enjoying a hearty legume stew, a salmon salad with nuts and seeds, or a colorful plate of roasted vegetables, these ingredients will nourish your heart and support your overall well-being.

Kitchen Tools and Equipment

To make heart-healthy cooking enjoyable and efficient, having the right tools and equipment in your kitchen is essential. Here's a list of recommended tools that will help you prepare nutritious meals with ease:

1. High-Quality Chef's Knife: A sharp, high-quality chef's knife is a must-have for any kitchen. It allows you to chop, slice, and dice ingredients efficiently, saving time and ensuring uniform cooking. A good chef's knife can handle a variety of tasks, from cutting vegetables to slicing lean meats.

2. Cutting Board: Invest in a sturdy, large cutting board to provide a stable surface for all your shopping needs. Opt for a board made of wood or plastic that is easy to clean and gentle on your knife. Consider having separate boards for raw meats and vegetables to prevent cross-contamination.

3. Measuring Cups and Spoons: Accurate measurements are crucial for heart-healthy cooking, especially when it comes to controlling portion sizes and sodium levels. A set of measuring cups and spoons will help you follow recipes precisely and maintain the nutritional integrity of your dishes.

4. Non-Stick Cookware: Non-stick pots and pans are ideal for heart-healthy cooking as they require less oil or fat for cooking, reducing the overall calorie and fat content of your meals. Invest in a high-quality non-stick skillet, saucepan, and baking sheet to cover a range of cooking methods.

5. Steamer Basket: A steamer basket allows you to cook vegetables, fish, and other ingredients without adding oil, preserving their nutrients and natural flavors. Steaming is a heart-healthy cooking method that helps retain vitamins and minerals while keeping food low in calories and fat.

6. Food Processor or Blender: A food processor or high-speed blender is invaluable for making smoothies, purees, sauces, and even chopping vegetables quickly. These appliances can help you incorporate more fruits and vegetables into your diet easily and prepare heart-healthy meals efficiently.

7. Slow Cooker or Instant Pot: These versatile appliances are perfect for preparing healthy, home-cooked meals with minimal effort. A slow cooker allows you to cook soups, stews, and lean meats slowly, enhancing flavors and tenderness. An Instant Pot combines the functions of a slow cooker, pressure cooker, and more, making it a multifunctional tool for heart-healthy cooking.

8. Digital Food Scale: A digital food scale is useful for portion control and ensuring you're using the right amounts of ingredients. This is especially important for heart-healthy cooking, where monitoring portion sizes and ingredient quantities can make a significant difference in the nutritional content of your meals.

9. Silicone Baking Mats: Silicone baking mats are a great alternative to parchment paper and can be reused multiple times. They provide a non-stick surface for baking without the need for additional oils or fats, making them ideal for heart-healthy baking.

10. Salad Spinner: A salad spinner makes it easy to wash and dry leafy greens and herbs, ensuring they are clean and ready to use in your heart-healthy salads and dishes. Properly dried greens also help dressings adhere better, enhancing the flavor of your salads.

11. Mason Jars and Storage Containers: Mason jars and airtight storage containers are perfect for meal prep and storing leftovers. Keeping your heart-healthy meals fresh and organized in the fridge or pantry ensures you always have nutritious options on hand.

By equipping your kitchen with these recommended tools, you'll find heart-healthy cooking more efficient and enjoyable. These tools not only save time and effort but also help you prepare meals that are delicious, nutritious, and supportive of your cardiovascular health. Happy cooking!

Simple cooking methods for beginners

Embarking on a journey to heart-healthy cooking doesn't have to be daunting, even for beginners. Mastering a few simple cooking methods can make a significant difference in your ability to prepare nutritious and delicious meals. Here are some basic cooking techniques that are easy to learn and perfect for creating heart-healthy dishes:

1. Steaming: Steaming is a gentle cooking method that preserves the nutrients and natural flavors of food. It involves cooking food with steam from boiling water. You can steam vegetables, fish, and even lean meats. Simply place a steamer basket over a pot of simmering water, add your ingredients, cover, and let the steam cook your food to tender perfection.

2. Sautéing: Sautéing involves cooking food quickly in a small amount of oil over medium-high heat. This method is perfect for vegetables, lean meats, and seafood. Use heart-healthy oils like olive oil or avocado oil. Heat the oil in a pan, add your ingredients, and cook until they are tender and lightly browned, stirring occasionally.

3. Roasting: Roasting is an excellent way to bring out the natural sweetness and flavors of vegetables and meats. Preheat your oven, lightly coat your ingredients with olive oil, season with herbs and spices, and spread them evenly on a baking sheet. Roast until they are golden brown and cooked through, turning halfway for even cooking.

4. Grilling: Grilling adds a delicious smoky flavor to your food without the need for added fats. You can grill vegetables, lean meats, and fish. Preheat your grill, lightly brush your ingredients with oil, and cook over medium-high heat until they have nice grill marks and are cooked to your desired doneness.

5. Boiling: Boiling is a straightforward method ideal for cooking grains, pasta, and vegetables. Bring a pot of water to a boil, add a pinch of salt, and cook your ingredients until they are tender. Drain and use as needed in your recipes.

6. Blanching: Blanching involves briefly boiling food and then plunging it into ice water to stop the cooking process. This technique is great for preserving the color and texture of vegetables. Use it to prepare vegetables for salads or as a step before freezing them.

7. Poaching: Poaching is a gentle cooking method where food is simmered in liquid at a low temperature. It's perfect for delicate foods like fish, eggs, and poultry. Bring a pot of water or broth to a simmer, add your ingredients, and cook gently until done.

8. Stir-Frying: Stir-frying is a quick and healthy way to cook small pieces of food over high heat with a small amount of oil. Use a wok or large skillet, heat the oil until hot, and stir-fry your ingredients until they are crisp-tender. This method is great for making nutritious and flavorful dishes with a variety of vegetables and proteins.

9. Baking: Baking is a versatile method used for making everything from main dishes to healthy desserts. Preheat your oven, follow the recipe instructions, and bake your ingredients until they are cooked through and golden brown.

10. Slow Cooking: Slow cooking is an easy way to prepare hearty, heart-healthy meals with minimal effort. Combine your ingredients in a slow cooker, set it to low or high, and let it cook for several hours. This method is perfect for soups, stews, and lean meats.

By mastering these simple cooking methods, you'll be well-equipped to prepare a variety of heart-healthy meals. Start with these basics and gradually expand your culinary skills as you gain confidence in the kitchen. Remember, cooking at home allows you to control the ingredients and make healthier choices, which is key to maintaining a heart-healthy diet. Happy cooking!

How to cook low-fat and low-sodium meals

Cooking low-fat and low-sodium meals is crucial for heart health, and it can be both simple and delicious with the right techniques. Here are some practical tips and methods to help you create flavorful and nutritious dishes while reducing fat and sodium:

1. Choose Lean Proteins: Opt for lean cuts of meat like chicken breast, turkey, and fish. Trim visible fat and remove skin before cooking. Plant-based proteins such as beans, lentils, and tofu are also excellent low-fat options.

2. Use Healthy Cooking Methods: Prefer cooking techniques that require little or no added fat. These methods help retain nutrients and natural flavors:

- **Grilling:** Adds a smoky flavor without extra fat.
- **Steaming:** Preserves vitamins and minerals, ideal for vegetables and fish.
- **Poaching:** Cooks food gently in water or broth, perfect for chicken and fish.
- **Baking:** Uses dry heat to cook food evenly with minimal added fat.
- **Stir-frying:** Uses a small amount of healthy oil like olive or avocado oil, ideal for vegetables and lean proteins.

3. Reduce Oil Usage: When sautéing or stir-frying, use non-stick cookware to minimize the amount of oil needed. Measure oil with a spoon to avoid overuse. Consider using cooking sprays as an alternative to reduce calories and fat.

4. Enhance Flavor Without Salt: To reduce sodium, explore other ways to add flavor:

- **Herbs and Spices:** Fresh or dried herbs like basil, oregano, thyme, and spices like paprika, cumin, and turmeric enhance flavor without adding sodium.
- **Citrus and Vinegar:** Lemon, lime, and vinegars (balsamic, apple cider) brighten dishes and add acidity.
- **Aromatics:** Garlic, onions, ginger, and fresh chilies add depth and complexity to meals.

5. Use Low-Sodium Alternatives: Choose low-sodium or no-salt-added versions of common ingredients:

- **Broths and Stocks:** Select low-sodium varieties or make your own to control salt levels.
- **Canned Goods:** Rinse canned beans and vegetables to reduce sodium content.
- **Soy Sauce:** Opt for low-sodium soy sauce or tamari.

6. Modify Recipes: Adjust recipes to reduce fat and sodium:

- **Dairy Substitutes:** Use low-fat or fat-free dairy products, or plant-based alternatives like almond milk or coconut yogurt.
- **Sauces and Dressings:** Make homemade versions using yogurt, vinegar, and fresh herbs to control ingredients and reduce added salt and fat.
- **Portion Control:** Smaller portions of high-fat and high-sodium foods can help manage intake without sacrificing flavor.

7. Incorporate Whole Foods: Base your meals around whole, unprocessed foods such as fruits, vegetables, whole grains, and legumes. These foods are naturally low in fat and sodium and high in essential nutrients.

8. Experiment with Cooking Techniques: Try methods that add flavor without fat or salt:

- **Roasting:** Enhances the natural sweetness of vegetables without added fat.
- **Smoking:** Adds a deep, rich flavor to meats and vegetables.
- **Infusing:** Use herb-infused oils or vinegars for a burst of flavor.

9. Be Mindful of Hidden Sodium and Fat: Check nutrition labels for hidden sources of sodium and fat in packaged foods. Look for terms like "partially hydrogenated oils" (trans fats) and "sodium benzoate" (preservative).

10. Plan Ahead: Prepare meals in advance to avoid the temptation of high-fat, high-sodium convenience foods. Batch-cook and freeze heart-healthy meals for busy days.

By implementing these strategies, you can enjoy delicious meals that are low in fat and sodium while supporting your heart health. Experiment with different techniques and ingredients to find what works best for your taste preferences **Chapter** and lifestyle. Happy, healthy cooking!

Breakfast Recipes

Smoothies and shakes

Starting your day with a nutritious smoothie or shake can be both quick and delicious. These beverages are versatile, easy to prepare, and packed with heart-healthy ingredients that provide essential nutrients, fiber, and antioxidants. Here are some simple and tasty recipes, along with tips to help you create your own heart-healthy smoothies and shakes:

Berry Banana Smoothie

Yield: 2 servings
Preparation Time: 10 minutes
Cooking Time: None

Ingredients:

- 150 grams of fresh or frozen mixed berries (blueberries, strawberries, raspberries)
- 1 medium banana (approximately 120 grams), sliced
- 240 milliliters of unsweetened almond milk (or any plant-based milk)
- 120 grams of plain Greek yogurt (use a dairy-free alternative for a vegan option)
- 1 tablespoon (12 grams) of chia seeds
- 1 tablespoon (7 grams) of ground flaxseed
- 1 teaspoon (5 milliliters) of honey or maple syrup (optional, for sweetness)
- 1 teaspoon (5 milliliters) of vanilla extract
- A handful of spinach leaves (optional for added nutrients)
- 6-8 ice cubes (optional, for a thicker smoothie)

Instructions:
Prepare the Ingredients: If using fresh berries, wash them thoroughly. If using frozen berries, there's no need to thaw. Slice the banana into chunks.
Measure out the almond milk and Greek yogurt.
Blend the Smoothie: In a high-speed blender, add the mixed berries, banana, almond milk, Greek yogurt, chia seeds, ground flaxseed, honey or maple syrup (if using), and vanilla extract.
For an extra nutrient boost, add a handful of spinach leaves.
Add ice cubes if a thicker, colder smoothie is desired.
Blend Until Smooth: Blend on high for about 1-2 minutes, or until the mixture is completely smooth and creamy.
If the smoothie is too thick, add a little more almond milk to reach the desired consistency. If it's too thin, add a few more ice cubes or a bit more yogurt.
Serve:
Pour the smoothie into two glasses.
Serve immediately to enjoy the fresh flavors and optimal nutrient content.

Nutritional Information (per serving):

Calories: 200
Total Fat: 5 g
Saturated Fat: 1g.
Trans Fat: 0 g., Cholesterol: 5 mg.
Sodium: 70 mg.
Total Carbohydrates: 32 g
Fiber: 7 g
Sugars: 19 g
Protein: 8 g

Greek Yogurt Parfait with Berries and Honey

Yield: 2 servings
Preparation Time: 10 minutes

Ingredients:

- 300 grams of plain Greek yogurt (low-fat or non-fat)
- 150 grams of mixed berries (blueberries, strawberries, raspberries)
- 30 grams of granola (low-sugar, whole grain)
- 20 grams of chopped nuts (almonds or walnuts)
- 1 tablespoon (15 milliliters) of honey
- 1 teaspoon (5 grams) of chia seeds (optional)
- 1 teaspoon (5 milliliters) of vanilla extract (optional)
- 1/2 teaspoon (2.5 grams) of ground cinnamon (optional)

Instructions :
Prepare the Ingredients: Wash and dry the berries. Hull and slice the strawberries if using. Measure out the Greek yogurt, granola, nuts, honey, chia seeds, vanilla extract, and ground cinnamon. Now, let's create a masterpiece. Layer the Parfait: In two serving glasses or bowls, start by adding a layer of Greek yogurt (approximately 100 grams per serving). Add a layer of mixed berries (about 75 grams per serving) on top of the yogurt. **Add Toppings:** Sprinkle half of the granola (15 grams per serving) over the berries. Add a portion of the chopped nuts (10 grams per serving) . If using, sprinkle a few chia seeds on top, **Drizzle with Drizzle half of the Honey**: honey (7.5 milliliters per serving) over the top of the parfait . Optionally, add a few drops of vanilla extract and a pinch of ground cinnamon for extra flavor. **Final Touch**: Add another dollop of Greek yogurt on top if desired, and finish with a few more berries and a final sprinkle of granola and nuts.

Nutritional Information (per serving):

Calories: 280
Total Fat: 8
Satureted Fat: 2 grams
Trans Fat: 0 grams
Cholesterol: 5 milligrams
Sodium: 55 milligrams
Total Carbohydrates: 36 gram
Dietary Fiber: 6 grams,
Sugars: 22 grams
Protein: 15 grams

Blueberry Chia Seed Pudding

Yield: 4 servings
Preparation Time: 5 minutes (plus chilling time)

Ingredients:

- 80 grams (1/2 cup) of chia seeds
- 480 milliliters (2 cups) of unsweetened almond milk
- 240 grams (1 1/2 cups) of fresh blueberries
- 30 milliliters (2 tablespoons) of pure maple syrup (optional)
- 5 milliliters (1 teaspoon) of vanilla extract
- Fresh blueberries, for serving
- Chopped nuts or seeds (such as almonds, walnuts, or pumpkin seeds), for serving

Instructions:

Prepare the Chia Seed Mixture: In a mixing bowl or large jar, combine the chia seeds and almond milk. Stir well to combine. Let the mixture sit for about 5 minutes, then stir again to prevent clumping. Blend the Blueberries: In a blender, combine the fresh blueberries, maple syrup (if using), and vanilla extract. Blend until smooth and creamy. Layer the Pudding: In serving glasses or jars, alternate layers of the chia seed mixture and the blended blueberry mixture. Start with a layer of chia seed mixture, followed by a layer of blueberry mixture, and continue until the glasses are filled.
Chill and Serve: Cover the glasses or jars with plastic wrap or lids and refrigerate for at least 2 hours, or preferably overnight, to allow the chia seeds to absorb the liquid and thicken. Before serving, top each pudding with fresh blueberries and chopped nuts or seeds for added texture and flavor.

Nutritional Information (per servings):

Calories: 180
Tota Saturated Fat: 3 grams
Saturated Fat: 8 grams
Cholesterol: 0 milligrams
Sodium: 60 milligrams
Total Carbohydrates: 21 grams
Dietary Fiber: 11grams
Sugars: 7grams
Protein: 5 grams

Mango and Pineapple Smoothie Bowl

Yield: 2 servings
Preparation Time: 10 minutes

Ingredients:

- 200 grams (1 1/2 cups) frozen mango chunks
- 150 grams (1 cup) frozen pineapple chunks
- 120 milliliters (1/2 cup) unsweetened almond milk
- 120 grams (1/2 cup) Greek yogurt
- 30 grams (2 tablespoons) chia seeds
- 30 grams (2 tablespoons) unsweetened shredded coconut
- 30 grams (1/4 cup) sliced almonds
- Fresh berries, for topping (optional)
- Honey or maple syrup, for drizzling (optional)

Instructions:
Blend the Smoothie Base:
In a blender, combine the frozen mango chunks, frozen pineapple chunks, almond milk, and Greek yogurt. Blend until smooth and creamy.
Prepare the Toppings:
In a small bowl, combine the chia seeds, shredded coconut, and sliced almonds.
Assemble the Smoothie Bowl:
Divide the smoothie mixture between two bowls.
Add Toppings:
Sprinkle the chia seed mixture evenly over the top of each smoothie bowl.
Garnish and Serve:
Garnish with fresh berries if desired, and drizzle with honey or maple syrup for a touch of sweetness
.
Nutritional Information (per serving):
Calories: 300
Total Fat: 12 grams
Saturated Fat: 3 grams
Trans Fat: 0 grams

Cholesterol: 0 milligrams
Total Carbohydrates: 40 grams
Dietary Fiber: 8 grams
Sugars: 28 grams
Protein: 10 grams

Protein-Packed Green Smoothie

Yield: 2 servings
Preparation Time: 5 minutes

Ingredients:

- 2 cups fresh spinach leaves (60 grams)
- 1 ripe banana (about 120 grams), peeled and sliced
- 1 cup unsweetened almond milk (240 milliliters)
- 1/2 cup plain Greek yogurt (120 grams)
- 1/4 cup rolled oats (20 grams)
- 2 tablespoons almond butter (30 grams)
- 1 tablespoon chia seeds (15 grams)
- 1 tablespoon honey (15 milliliters), optional for sweetness
- 1/2 teaspoon vanilla extract (2.5 milliliters)
- Ice cubes (optional)

Instructions:
Prepare the Ingredients:
Wash the spinach leaves thoroughly and pat them dry with paper towels.
Peel and slice the ripe banana.
Blend the Ingredients:
In a blender, combine the spinach leaves, sliced banana, almond milk, Greek yogurt, rolled oats, almond butter, chia seeds, honey (if using), and vanilla extract.
If desired, add a few ice cubes to the blender to make the smoothie colder.
Blend Until Smooth:
Blend the ingredients on high speed until smooth and creamy, scraping down the sides of the blender as needed.
Adjust Consistency:
If the smoothie is too thick, add more almond milk, a tablespoon at a time, until you reach your desired consistency.
Serve Immediately:
Pour the protein-packed green smoothie into glasses and serve immediately.

Nutritional Information (per serving):
Calories: 250
Total Fat: 10 grams
Saturated Fat: 1 gram
Trans Fat: 0 grams
Cholesterol: 0 milligrams
Sodium: 120 milligrams
Total Carbohydrates: 30 grams
Dietary Fiber: 6 grams
Sugars: 12 grams
Protein: 12 grams

Overnight oats and porridges

Overnight oats and porridges are excellent breakfast options for those seeking quick, easy, and heart-healthy meals. These dishes can be prepared in advance and customized to suit your taste preferences and nutritional needs. Here are delicious recipe and tips to help you incorporate overnight oats and porridges into your breakfast routine:

Apple Cinnamon Overnight Oats

Yield: 2 servings
Preparation Time: 10 minutes
Cooking Time: Overnight refrigeration (minimum 6 hours)

Ingredients:

- 100 grams of rolled oats
- 240 milliliters of unsweetened almond milk (or any plant-based milk)
- 1 medium apple (approximately 150 grams), chopped
- 1 tablespoon (10 grams) of chia seeds
- 1 tablespoon (7 grams) of ground flaxseed
- 1/2 teaspoon (1 gram) of ground cinnamon
- 1/4 teaspoon (1.5 grams) of vanilla extract
- 1 tablespoon (15 milliliters) of maple syrup or honey (optional, for sweetness)
- 20 grams of chopped walnuts or almonds (optional, for added healthy fats)
- **A pinch of salt (optional)**

Instructions:
Prepare the Ingredients:
Chop the apple into small pieces, removing the core and seeds.
Measure out the oats, almond milk, chia seeds, ground flaxseed, cinnamon, and vanilla extract.
Mix the Ingredients:
In a medium-sized bowl or a jar with a lid, combine the rolled oats, chia seeds, ground flaxseed, and ground cinnamon. Add the chopped apple to the bowl.
Pour in the almond milk, vanilla extract, and maple syrup or honey (if using). Stir well to ensure all ingredients are thoroughly mixed.
Add Toppings:
If using, add the chopped walnuts or almonds on top of the mixture.
A pinch of salt can be added to enhance the flavor, but this is optional.
Refrigerate Overnight:
Cover the bowl or jar with a lid or plastic wrap.
Refrigerate the mixture overnight or for at least 6 hours to allow the oats and chia seeds to absorb the liquid and soften
Serve:
In the morning, give the oats a good stir to combine any settled ingredients.
If the mixture is too thick, you can add a splash of almond milk to reach your desired consistency.
Serve cold directly from the fridge or heat it in the microwave for 1-2 minutes if you prefer a warm breakfast
.

Nutritional Information (per serving):

Calories: 320
Total Fat: 10 grams
Saturated Fat: 1 gram
Trans Fat: 0 grams
Cholesterol: 0 milligrams
Sodium: 60 milligrams
Total Carbohydrates: 50 grams
Dietary Fiber: 10 grams
Sugars: 15 grams
Protein: 8 grams

Heart-Healthy Egg Dishes

Eggs are a versatile and nutritious option for heart-healthy breakfasts. They are a great source of high-quality protein, vitamins, and minerals while being low in calories. Here are some delicious and heart-healthy scrambled, boiled, and baked egg recipes to start your day right:

Spinach and Mushroom Omelette

Yield: 2 servings
Preparation Time: 10 minutes
Cooking Time: 10 minutes

Ingredients:

- 100 grams of fresh spinach leaves
- 100 grams of mushrooms, sliced
- 4 large eggs (approximately 240 grams)
- 60 milliliters of skim milk or unsweetened almond milk
- 1 tablespoon (15 milliliters) of olive oil
- 1 small onion (about 50 grams), finely chopped
- 1 clove garlic (about 5 grams), minced
- 1 tablespoon (15 grams) of grated Parmesan cheese (optional)
- 1 tablespoon (5 grams) of chopped fresh parsley
- 1/4 teaspoon (1.5 grams) of black pepper
- 1/4 teaspoon (1.5 grams) of salt (optional or to taste)

Instructions:

Prepare the Ingredients:
Wash and dry the spinach leaves. Slice the mushrooms. Finely chop the onion and mince the garlic.
Sauté the Vegetables:
Heat 1/2 tablespoon (7.5 milliliters) of olive oil in a non-stick skillet over medium heat.
Add the onions and cook until translucent, about 2-3 minutes.
Add the mushrooms and garlic, and sauté until the mushrooms are tender and have released their moisture, about 4-5 minutes.
Add the spinach and cook until wilted, about 1-2 minutes. Remove the mixture from the skillet and set aside.
Prepare the Egg Mixture:
In a medium bowl, whisk together the eggs, milk, black pepper, and salt (if using).
Cook the Omelette:
Heat the remaining 1/2 tablespoon (7.5 milliliters) of olive oil in the same skillet over medium heat.
Pour half of the egg mixture into the skillet, tilting the pan to spread the eggs evenly.
Cook until the eggs begin to set around the edges, about 2-3 minutes.
Add the Filling:
Spoon half of the spinach and mushroom mixture over one half of the omelette.
Sprinkle with a bit of Parmesan cheese (if using) and chopped parsley.
Fold and Finish:
Carefully fold the omelette in half to cover the filling.
Cook for another 1-2 minutes until the eggs are fully set.
Slide the omelette onto a plate and repeat with the remaining ingredients to make a second omelette.

Nutritional Information (per serving):
Calories: 220
Total Fat: 14 grams
Saturated Fat: 3 grams
Trans Fat: 0 grams
Cholesterol: 285 milligrams
Sodium: 250 milligrams
Total Carbohydrates: 5 grams

Dietary Fiber: 2 grams
Sugars: 2 grams
Protein: 18 grams

.

Avocado Toast with Poached Egg

Yield: 2 servings
Preparation Time: 10 minutes
Cooking Time: 10 minutes

Ingredients:

- 2 slices of whole grain bread (approximately 60 grams)
- 1 ripe avocado (approximately 150 grams)
- 2 large eggs (approximately 100 grams)
- 1 tablespoon (15 milliliters) of lemon juice
- 1 tablespoon (15 grams) of chopped fresh cilantro or parsley
- 1/4 teaspoon (1 gram) of ground black pepper
- 1/4 teaspoon (1 gram) of red pepper flakes (optional)
- A pinch of salt (optional, preferably sea salt)
- 1 teaspoon (5 milliliters) of olive oil (optional, for drizzling)
- Water for poaching

Instructions:
Prepare the Ingredients:
Toast the slices of whole grain bread until they are golden brown.
Halve and pit the avocado, then scoop the flesh into a bowl. Mash the avocado with a fork until smooth.
Add the lemon juice, chopped cilantro or parsley, ground black pepper, and optional red pepper flakes to the mashed avocado. Mix well.
Poach the Eggs:
Fill a medium saucepan with water and bring it to a gentle simmer.
Crack each egg into a small bowl or ramekin.
Create a gentle whirlpool in the water using a spoon, then carefully slide each egg into the water. Poach the eggs for about 3-4 minutes for a runny yolk, or longer if a firmer yolk is desired.
Remove the poached eggs with a slotted spoon and place them on a paper towel to drain excess water.
Assemble the Avocado Toast:
Spread the mashed avocado mixture evenly on each slice of toasted whole grain bread.
Place a poached egg on top of the avocado on each slice of toast.
Final Touch:
Drizzle a small amount of olive oil over the top (optional) for added healthy fats.
Sprinkle a pinch of salt if desired and add extra chopped herbs or red pepper flakes for garnish.

Nutritional Information (per serving):
Calories: 300
Total Fat: 20 grams
Saturated Fat: 3 grams
Trans Fat: 0 grams
Cholesterol: 185 milligrams
Sodium: 180 milligrams
Total Carbohydrates: 23 grams
Dietary Fiber: 9 grams
Sugars: 2 grams
Protein: 12 grams

Egg White and Veggie Frittata

Yield: 4 servings
Preparation Time: 15 minutes
Cooking Time: 25 minutes

Ingredients:

- 8 large egg whites
- 120 milliliters (1/2 cup) unsweetened almond milk
- 100 grams (1 cup) cherry tomatoes, halved
- 100 grams (1 cup) baby spinach, chopped
- 1/2 medium red bell pepper, diced
- 1/2 medium yellow bell pepper, diced
- 1/2 medium red onion, diced
- 60 grams (1/2 cup) reduced-fat feta cheese, crumbled
- 5 milliliters (1 teaspoon) olive oil

- 2 cloves garlic, minced
- 5 milliliters (1 teaspoon) dried oregano
- Salt and pepper to taste
- Cooking spray

Instructions:

Preheat the Oven:
Preheat your oven to 180°C (350°F).

Prepare the Vegetables:
Heat the olive oil in a skillet over medium heat. Add the diced red onion and bell peppers, and sauté for 3-4 minutes, until softened.
Add the minced garlic and chopped spinach to the skillet, and cook for an additional 1-2 minutes, until the spinach wilts. Remove from heat and set aside.

Whisk the Egg Mixture:
In a mixing bowl, whisk together the egg whites, unsweetened almond milk, dried oregano, salt, and pepper until well combined.
Assemble the Frittata:

Lightly grease an oven-safe skillet or baking dish with cooking spray. Transfer the sautéed vegetables to the skillet, spreading them out evenly.
Pour the egg white mixture over the vegetables in the skillet. Arrange the halved cherry tomatoes on top, and sprinkle the crumbled feta cheese over the mixture.

Bake the Frittata:
Place the skillet or baking dish in the preheated oven and bake for 20-25 minutes, or until the frittata is set and golden brown on top.

Serve and Enjoy:
Once baked, remove the frittata from the oven and let it cool slightly before slicing.
Serve warm slices of the egg white and veggie frittata with a side salad or whole grain toast for a complete and heart-healthy meal.

Nutritional Information (per serving):

Calories: 120
Total Fat: 5 grams
Saturated Fat: 2 grams
Trans Fat: 0 grams
Cholesterol: 5 milligrams

Sodium: 320 milligrams
Total Carbohydrates: 6 grams
Dietary Fiber: 2 grams
Sugars: 3 grams
Protein: 15 grams

Tomato and Avocado Breakfast Sandwich

Yield: 2 servings
Preparation Time: 10 minutes
Cooking Time: 5 minutes

Ingredients:

- 4 slices whole grain bread
- 1 ripe avocado, peeled, pitted, and thinly sliced
- 1 large tomato, thinly sliced
- 2 large eggs
- 60 grams (about 1/2 cup) baby spinach leaves
- 1 tablespoon olive oil
- Salt and pepper to taste

Instructions:

Prepare the Ingredients:
Thinly slice the avocado and tomato. Wash the baby spinach leaves and pat them dry with paper towels.

Cook the Eggs:
Heat a non-stick skillet over medium heat and add 1/2 tablespoon of olive oil.
Crack the eggs into the
skillet and cook to your desired doneness (sunny-side-up over-easy, or scrambled).

Toast the Bread:
While the eggs are cooking,
toast the whole grain bread slices until lightly golden brown.

Assemble the Sandwiches:
On two slices of toasted bread, layer the avocado slices, followed by the tomato slices.
Top each sandwich with cooked eggs and baby spinach leaves.
Season with salt and pepper to taste.

Close the Sandwiches:
Place the remaining two slices of toasted bread on top of each sandwich to close.
Serve Warm:
Serve the tomato and avocado breakfast sandwiches immediately while warm.

Nutritional Information (per serving):

Calories: 320
Total Fat: 20 grams
Saturated Fat: 3 grams
Trans Fat: 0 grams
Sugars: 4 grams

Cholesterol: 185 milligrams
Sodium: 220 milligrams
Total Carbohydrates: 28 grams
Dietary Fiber: 8 grams
Protein: 12 grams

Delicious and Nutritious Breakfast Bowls

Fruit and yogurt bowls are a delightful way to start your day with a nutritious and delicious breakfast. These bowls combine the creamy texture of yogurt with the natural sweetness of fresh fruits, creating a balanced meal rich in protein, fiber, vitamins, and minerals. Here are some recipes and tips for making the perfect fruit and yogurt bowls:

Quinoa Breakfast Bowl with Fresh Fruit

Yield: 2 servings
Preparation Time: 10 minutes
Cooking Time: 15 minutes

Ingredients:

- 100 grams of quinoa
- 240 milliliters of water
- 1 tablespoon (15 milliliters) of honey or maple syrup (optional)
- 150 grams of mixed fresh fruits (such as berries, apple slices, and banana)
- 2 tablespoons (30 grams) of plain Greek yogurt
- 1 tablespoon (10 grams) of chia seeds
- 1 tablespoon (10 grams) of flaxseeds
- 1 teaspoon (5 grams) of ground cinnamon
- 1 teaspoon (5 grams) of vanilla extract (optional)
- 15 grams of chopped nuts (such as almonds or walnuts)

Instructions:

Prepare the Quinoa:
Rinse the quinoa under cold water using a fine-mesh sieve.
In a medium saucepan, combine the rinsed quinoa and water. Bring to a boil over medium-high heat.
Reduce the heat to low, cover, and simmer for about 15 minutes or until the water is absorbed and the quinoa is tender.
Remove from heat and let it sit, covered, for 5 minutes. Fluff with a fork.
Sweeten and Flavor the Quinoa (Optional):
If desired, stir in the honey or maple syrup, ground cinnamon, and vanilla extract into the warm quinoa for added flavor and sweetness.

Assemble the Breakfast Bowls:
Divide the cooked quinoa evenly between two bowls.
Top each bowl with mixed fresh fruits, arranging them neatly for an appealing presentation.
Add a dollop of plain Greek yogurt to each bowl.
Sprinkle chia seeds, flaxseeds, and chopped nuts over the top for: added texture and nutrients.
Final Touch:
For an extra touch of sweetness and a hint of spice, sprinkle a little more ground cinnamon on top of the bowls if desired.

Nutritional Information (per serving):
Calories: 350
Total Fat: 10 grams
Saturated Fat: 1 gram
Trans Fat: 0 grams
Cholesterol: 0 milligrams

Sodium: 30 milligrams
Total Carbohydrates: 55 grams
Dietary Fiber: 10 grams
Sugars: 20 grams
Protein: 12 grams

Cottage Cheese and Peach Breakfast Bowl

Yield: 2 servings
Preparation Time: 10 minutes
Cooking Time: 0 minutes

Ingredients:

- 200 grams (1 cup) low-fat cottage cheese
- 2 medium peaches, sliced
- 30 grams (2 tablespoons) chopped walnuts
- 15 milliliters (1 tablespoon) honey
- 5 milliliters (1 teaspoon) vanilla extract
- 5 milliliters (1 teaspoon) ground cinnamon

Instructions:

Prepare the Cottage Cheese Base:
In a mixing bowl, combine the low-fat cottage cheese, honey, and vanilla extract. Mix well until the ingredients are evenly incorporated.

Assemble the Breakfast Bowl:
Divide the cottage cheese mixture evenly between two serving bowls.

Add Sliced Peaches:
Arrange the sliced peaches on top of the cottage cheese in each bowl.

Sprinkle with Walnuts:
Sprinkle the chopped walnuts over the peaches in each bowl.

Finish with Cinnamon:
Lightly dust each breakfast bowl with ground cinnamon for added flavor.

Serve and Enjoy:
Serve the cottage cheese and peach breakfast bowls immediately, or cover and refrigerate for a refreshing breakfast on the go.

Nutritional Information (per serving):

Calories: 220
Total Fat: 7 grams
Saturated Fat: 1 gram
Trans Fat: 0 grams
Cholesterol: 10 milligrams
Sodium: 280 milligrams
Total Carbohydrates: 25 grams
Dietary Fiber: 3 grams
Sugars: 20 grams
Protein: 15 grams

Savory grain bowls

Savory grain bowls are a fantastic way to enjoy a hearty and nutritious breakfast that breaks the mold of traditional sweet morning meals. These bowls are versatile, allowing you to incorporate a variety of grains, vegetables, and proteins to create a balanced and delicious start to your day. Here are some savory grain bowl recipes and tips to help you get started:

Veggie-Packed Breakfast Burrito

Yield: 2 servings
Preparation Time: 15 minutes
Cooking Time: 10 minutes

Ingredients:

- Two whole-wheat tortillas (about 60 grams each)
- One tablespoon (15 milliliters) of olive oil
- 100 grams of baby spinach
- One small bell pepper (red or yellow), diced (about 100 grams)
- One small zucchini, diced (about 100 grams)
- 100 grams of mushrooms, sliced
- Four large egg whites (about 120 grams)
- One small avocado, sliced (about 150 grams)
- 30 grams of low-fat shredded cheese
- Two tablespoons (30 grams) of salsa (low-sodium if available)
- One teaspoon (5 grams) of ground cumin
- One teaspoon (5 grams) of paprika
- 1/2 teaspoon (2.5 grams) of garlic powder
- 1/2 teaspoon (2.5 grams) of black pepper

Instructions:

Prepare the Vegetables:

Heat the olive oil over medium heat in a large, non-stick skillet.

Add the diced bell pepper, zucchini, and sliced mushrooms to the skillet. Sauté for about 5-7 minutes until the vegetables are tender.

Add Spinach and Seasonings:

Add the baby spinach to the skillet and cook until wilted about 2 minutes.

Sprinkle the ground cumin, paprika, garlic powder, and black pepper over the vegetables. Stir well to combine.

Cook the Egg Whites:

Push the vegetables to one side of the skillet and pour the egg whites into the other.

Nutritional Information (per serving):

Calories: 350
Total Fat: 15 grams
Saturated Fat: 3 grams
Trans Fat: 0 grams
Cholesterol: 0 milligrams

Scramble the egg whites for about 2-3 minutes until fully cooked, then mix them with the vegetables.

Assemble the Burritos:

To make the whole-wheat tortillas more pliable, warm them in the microwave for about 15 seconds or in a dry skillet for 30 seconds on each side.

Divide the vegetable and egg white mixture evenly between the two tortillas.

Top each with slices of avocado, a sprinkle of low-fat shredded cheese, and a tablespoon of salsa.

Wrap the Burritos:

Fold the sides of the tortilla over the filling, then roll it up tightly from the bottom to the top. Slice each burrito in half for easier handling.

Sodium: 400 milligrams
Total Carbohydrates: 35 grams
Dietary Fiber: 10 grams
Sugars: 4 grams
Protein: 20 grams

Sweet Potato and Black Bean Hash

Yield: 4 servings
Preparation Time: 10 minutes
Cooking Time: 25 minutes

Ingredients:

- 500 grams (2 medium) sweet potatoes, peeled and diced
- 240 grams (1 can) black beans, drained and rinsed
- 1 medium red bell pepper, diced
- 1 small red onion, finely chopped

- 2 cloves garlic, minced
- 15 milliliters (1 tablespoon) olive oil
- 5 milliliters (1 teaspoon) ground cumin
- 5 milliliters (1 teaspoon) smoked paprika
- Salt and pepper to taste
- Fresh cilantro or parsley, chopped (for garnish)

Instructions:

Prepare the Sweet Potatoes:

Place the diced sweet potatoes in a microwave-safe bowl and microwave on high for 3-4 minutes, or until slightly softened. This will help reduce the cooking time.

Sauté the Vegetables:

In a large skillet, heat the olive oil over medium heat.

Add the diced red bell pepper and chopped red onion, and cook for 3-4 minutes, or until softened.

Add the minced garlic, ground cumin, and smoked paprika to the skillet. Cook for an additional 1-2 minutes, or until fragrant.

Cook the Sweet Potato Hash:

Add the partially cooked sweet potatoes to the skillet with the sautéed vegetables. Stir to combine.

Cook for 12-15 minutes, stirring occasionally, until the sweet potatoes are tender and lightly browned.

Add the Black Beans:

Once the sweet potatoes are cooked through, add the drained and rinsed black beans to the skillet. Stir gently to combine.

Cook for an additional 2-3 minutes, or until the beans are heated through.

Season and Serve:

Season the sweet potato and black bean hash with salt and pepper to taste.

Garnish with freshly chopped cilantro or parsley before serving.

Nutritional Information (per serving):

Calories: 220
Total Fat: 4 grams

Saturated Fat: 0.5 grams
Trans Fat: 0 grams
Cholesterol: 0 milligrams

Sodium: 200 milligrams
Total Carbohydrates: 40 grams
Dietary Fiber: 10 grams

Sugars: 6 grams
Protein: 8 grams

Savory Oatmeal with Spinach and Parmesan

Yield: 2 servings
Preparation Time: 10 minutes
Cooking Time: 15 minutes

Ingredients:

- 100 grams (1 cup) rolled oats
- 300 milliliters (1 1/4 cups) water
- 120 milliliters (1/2 cup) low-sodium vegetable broth
- 100 grams (about 2 cups) fresh spinach, chopped
- 30 grams (1/4 cup) grated Parmesan cheese
- 15 milliliters (1 tablespoon) olive oil
- 2 cloves garlic, minced
- Salt and pepper to taste

Instructions:

Cook the Oatmeal:
In a saucepan, bring the water and vegetable broth to a boil over medium heat.
Stir in the rolled oats and reduce the heat to low. Simmer for 10-15 minutes, stirring occasionally, until the oats are tender and the liquid is absorbed.
Prepare the Spinach:
While the oatmeal is cooking, heat olive oil in a skillet over medium heat. Add the minced garlic and cook for 1-2 minutes until fragrant.
Add the chopped spinach to the skillet and sauté for 2-3 minutes until wilted. Season with salt and pepper to taste.

Combine the Ingredients:
Once the oatmeal is cooked, stir in the sautéed spinach until well combined.
Serve with Parmesan:
Divide the savory oatmeal between two serving bowls. Sprinkle grated Parmesan cheese over the top of each bowl.
Garnish and Enjoy:
Garnish with additional black pepper or a drizzle of olive oil if desired. Serve the savory oatmeal warm and enjoy!

Nutritional Information (per serving):

Calories: 250
Total Fat: 10 grams
Saturated Fat: 3 grams
Trans Fat: 0 grams
Cholesterol: 10 milligrams

Sodium: 200 milligrams
Total Carbohydrates: 30 grams
Dietary Fiber: 5 grams
Sugars: 1 gram
Protein: 10 grams

Whole Grains and Baked Goods

Whole grains and baked goods provide a nutritious and satisfying start to the day, offering several benefits essential for a heart-healthy diet. These recipes typically include ingredients like whole wheat flour, oats, and nuts, which are rich in fiber, vitamins, and minerals. Versatile and Delicious: This group offers a range of tasty and satisfying options that can be customized to suit individual preferences and dietary needs. Whether it's the hearty crunch of granola, the comforting warmth of baked French toast, or the fluffiness of pancakes and waffles, there's something to appeal to everyone.

Almond Butter and Banana Whole Wheat Pancakes

Yield: 4 servings
Preparation Time: 10 minutes
Cooking Time: 15 minutes

Ingredients:

- 1 large ripe banana (about 120 grams)
- 2 large eggs (about 100 grams)
- 240 milliliters of unsweetened almond milk
- 1 teaspoon (5 milliliters) of vanilla extract
- 2 tablespoons (30 grams) of almond butter

- 150 grams of whole wheat flour
- 1 tablespoon (15 grams) of baking powder
- 1/2 teaspoon (2.5 grams) of ground cinnamon
- 1/4 teaspoon (1.25 grams) of salt
- Cooking spray or a small amount of olive oil for greasing the pan

Instructions:

Prepare the Wet Ingredients:
In a medium bowl, mash the banana until smooth. Add the eggs, almond milk, vanilla extract, and almond butter. Whisk until well combined.
Prepare the Dry Ingredients:
In a separate large bowl, combine the whole wheat flour, baking powder, ground cinnamon, and salt. Mix well. Combine Wet and Dry Ingredients:
Pour the wet ingredients into the dry ingredients. Stir gently until just combined. Be careful not to overmix; it's okay if there are a few lumps.
Cook the Pancakes:

Heat a non-stick skillet or griddle over medium heat. Lightly grease with cooking spray or a small amount of olive oil.
Pour 60 milliliters (1/4 cup) of batter onto the skillet for each pancake. Cook until bubbles form on the surface and the edges look set, about 2-3 minutes.
Flip the pancakes and cook for an additional 2-3 minutes until golden brown and cooked through. Repeat with the remaining batter.
Serve:
Serve the pancakes warm, optionally topped with additional sliced bananas, a drizzle of almond butter, or a sprinkle of fresh berries.

Nutritional Information (per serving):

Calories: 270
Total Fat: 10 grams
Saturated Fat: 1 gram
Trans Fat: 0 grams
Cholesterol: 55 milligrams

Sodium: 350 milligrams
Total Carbohydrates: 35 grams
Dietary Fiber: 5 grams
Sugars: 9 grams
Protein: 9 grams

Steel-Cut Oats with Nuts and Dried Fruit

Yield: 4 servings
Preparation Time: 5 minutes
Cooking Time: 30 minutes

Ingredients:

- 160 grams (1 cup) of steel-cut oats
- 720 milliliters (3 cups) of water
- 240 milliliters (1 cup) of unsweetened almond milk
- 40 grams (1/4 cup) of chopped almonds
- 40 grams (1/4 cup) of chopped walnuts

- 40 grams (1/4 cup) of dried cranberries
- 40 grams (1/4 cup) of raisins
- 1 tablespoon (15 milliliters) of maple syrup (optional)
- 1/2 teaspoon (2.5 milliliters) of vanilla extract
- 1/2 teaspoon (2.5 grams) of ground cinnamon
- Pinch of salt

Instructions:

Cook the Steel-Cut Oats:
In a medium saucepan, bring the water to a boil. Stir in the steel-cut oats and reduce the heat to low. Simmer, uncovered, for 20-25 minutes, stirring occasionally, until the oats are tender and have absorbed most of the water.
Add Almond Milk and Flavorings:

Stir in the almond milk, chopped almonds, chopped walnuts, dried cranberries, raisins, maple syrup (if using), vanilla extract, ground cinnamon, and a pinch of salt.
Simmer and Serve:
Continue to simmer the oats for an additional 5-10 minutes, until the mixture thickens to your desired consistency and the flavors meld together.
Remove from heat and let it sit for a few minutes to cool slightly.

Serve Warm:
Divide the steel-cut oats into serving bowls.

Nutritional Information (per serving):

Calories: 320
Total Fat: 11 grams
Saturated Fat: 1 gram
Trans Fat: 0 grams
Cholesterol: 0 milligrams

Sodium: 50 milligrams
Total Carbohydrates: 47 grams
Dietary Fiber: 7 grams
Sugars: 13 grams
Protein: 9 grams

Optionally, garnish with additional nuts, dried fruit, or a drizzle of maple syrup.
Serve warm and enjoy!

Heart-Healthy Granola with Almond Milk

Yield: 8 servings
Preparation Time: 10 minutes
Cooking Time: 25 minutes

Ingredients:

- 200 grams (2 cups) old-fashioned rolled oats
- 60 grams (1/2 cup) almonds, chopped
- 60 grams (1/2 cup) walnuts, chopped
- 30 grams (1/4 cup) pumpkin seeds
- 30 grams (1/4 cup) sunflower seeds
- 30 grams (1/4 cup) unsweetened shredded coconut
- 60 milliliters (1/4 cup) pure maple syrup
- 30 milliliters (2 tablespoons) coconut oil, melted
- 5 milliliters (1 teaspoon) vanilla extract
- 2.5 milliliters (1/2 teaspoon) ground cinnamon
- Pinch of salt
- 480 milliliters (2 cups) unsweetened almond milk, for serving

Instructions:
Preheat the Oven:
Preheat your oven to 160°C (325°F) and line a baking sheet with parchment paper.
Prepare the Granola Mixture:
In a large mixing bowl, combine the rolled oats, chopped almonds, chopped walnuts, pumpkin seeds, sunflower seeds, and unsweetened shredded coconut. Mix well to combine.
Sweeten and Flavor the Granola:
In a small bowl, whisk together the pure maple syrup, melted coconut oil, vanilla extract, ground cinnamon, and a pinch of salt.
Pour the maple syrup mixture over the dry ingredients and stir until everything is well coated.
Bake the Granola:

Spread the granola mixture evenly onto the prepared baking sheet.
Bake in the preheated oven for 20-25 minutes, stirring halfway through, until the granola is golden brown and crisp.
Cool and Store:
Allow the granola to cool completely on the baking sheet. It will crisp up further as it cools.
Once cooled, transfer the granola to an airtight container for storage.
Serve with Almond Milk:
To serve, divide the heart-healthy granola into bowls and pour unsweetened almond milk over the top.
Enjoy your heart-healthy breakfast or snack!

Nutritional Information (per serving, granola only):

Calories: 250
Total Fat: 16 grams
Saturated Fat: 5 grams
Trans Fat: 0 grams
Cholesterol: 0 milligrams

Sodium: 10 milligrams
Total Carbohydrates: 22 grams
Dietary Fiber: 4 grams
Sugars: 5 grams
Protein: 6 gram

Whole Grain Waffles with Fresh Berries

Yield: 4 servings

Preparation Time: 15 minutes
Cooking Time: 15 minutes

Ingredients:

- 120 grams (1 cup) whole wheat flour
- 30 grams (1/4 cup) ground flaxseed
- 10 grams (2 teaspoons) baking powder
- 2 grams (1/2 teaspoon) ground cinnamon
- 240 milliliters (1 cup) unsweetened almond milk
- 30 milliliters (2 tablespoons) maple syrup
- 15 milliliters (1 tablespoon) olive oil
- 5 milliliters (1 teaspoon) vanilla extract
- 2 large eggs, separated
- Cooking spray
- Fresh berries (such as strawberries, blueberries, raspberries) for serving
- Greek yogurt or low-fat yogurt for serving

Instructions:

Preheat the Waffle Iron:
Preheat your waffle iron according to the manufacturer's instructions.

Prepare the Dry Ingredients:
In a large mixing bowl, whisk together the whole wheat flour, ground flaxseed, baking powder, and ground cinnamon until well combined.

Mix the Wet Ingredients:
In a separate bowl, combine the almond milk, maple syrup, olive oil, vanilla extract, and egg yolks. Whisk until smooth.

Combine Wet and Dry Ingredients:
Gradually pour the wet ingredients into the dry ingredients, stirring until just combined. Be careful not to overmix.

Beat the Egg Whites:

In a clean bowl, use an electric mixer to beat the egg whites until stiff peaks form.

Fold in Egg Whites:
Gently fold the beaten egg whites into the batter until evenly incorporated. This will help make the waffles light and fluffy.

Cook the Waffles:
Lightly coat the preheated waffle iron with cooking spray.
Pour the batter onto the waffle iron, spreading it out evenly. Close the lid and cook according to the manufacturer's instructions, until the waffles are golden brown and crisp.

Serve with Fresh Berries and Yogurt:
Serve the whole grain waffles warm, topped with fresh berries and a dollop of Greek yogurt or low-fat yogurt.

Nutritional Information (per serving):

Calories: 250
Total Fat: 8 grams
Saturated Fat: 1 gram
Trans Fat: 0 grams
Cholesterol: 95 milligrams

Sodium: 350 milligrams
Total Carbohydrates: 36 grams
Dietary Fiber: 6 grams
Sugars: 7 grams
Protein: 10 gram

Baked Apple Cinnamon French Toast

Yield: 6 servings
Preparation Time: 20 minutes
Cooking Time: 40 minutes

Ingredients:

- 6 slices whole grain bread, preferably whole wheat (about 300 grams)
- 3 medium apples, peeled, cored, and thinly sliced
- 4 large eggs
- 240 milliliters (1 cup) unsweetened almond milk
- 60 milliliters (1/4 cup) pure maple syrup
- 1 teaspoon ground cinnamon
- 1/2 teaspoon vanilla extract
- Pinch of salt
- Cooking spray or olive oil, for greasing

Instructions:

Preheat the Oven:
Preheat your oven to 180°C (350°F). Lightly grease a 9x13-inch baking dish with cooking spray or olive oil.

Prepare the Bread and Apples:
Arrange the whole grain bread slices in a single layer in the prepared baking dish.

Layer the thinly sliced apples evenly over the bread slices.

Whisk the Egg Mixture:
In a medium mixing bowl, whisk together the eggs, almond milk, maple syrup, ground cinnamon, vanilla extract, and a pinch of salt until well combined.

Pour the Egg Mixture:
Pour the egg mixture evenly over the bread and apples in the baking dish, ensuring that all the bread is soaked.

Bake the French Toast:
Transfer the baking dish to the preheated oven and bake for 35-40 minutes, or until the French toast is golden brown and set in the center.

Serve Warm:
Once baked, remove the French toast from the oven and let it cool slightly before serving. Slice into portions and serve warm.

Nutritional Information (per serving):

Calories: 220
Total Fat: 6 grams
Saturated Fat: 1.5 grams
Trans Fat: 0 grams
Cholesterol: 140 milligrams

Sodium: 220 milligrams
Total Carbohydrates: 35 grams
Dietary Fiber: 5 grams
Sugars: 15 grams
Protein: 9 grams

Lunch Recipes

Variety of salad recipes

Incorporating a variety of salad recipes into your lunch routine is a delicious way to enjoy a nutritious and satisfying meal. Salads offer endless possibilities for combining fresh ingredients, flavors, and textures, making them versatile and customizable to suit your preferences. Here are some simple and flavorful salad recipes to inspire your lunchtime creations:

Quinoa and Black Bean Salad

Yield: 4 servings
Preparation Time: 15 minutes
Cooking Time: 20 minutes

Ingredients

- **Quinoa:**
- 200 grams quinoa
- 480 milliliters water
- **Salad:**
- 1 can (400 grams) black beans, rinsed and drained
- 1 red bell pepper, diced (150 grams)
- 1 yellow bell pepper, diced (150 grams)
- 1 small red onion, finely chopped (70 grams)
- 200 grams cherry tomatoes, halved
- 1 avocado, diced (150 grams)
- 15 grams fresh cilantro, chopped

- 1 teaspoon ground cumin
- 1 teaspoon chili powder
- 1 teaspoon smoked paprika
- **Dressing:**
- 60 milliliters extra-virgin olive oil
- 60 milliliters freshly squeezed lime juice (about 2 limes)
- 1 tablespoon honey (20 grams)
- 1 clove garlic, minced
- 1/2 teaspoon salt
- 1/4 teaspoon black pepper

Instructions:
Cook the Quinoa:
Rinse the quinoa under cold water to remove any bitterness.
In a medium saucepan, combine quinoa and water. Bring to a boil over medium-high heat.
Reduce heat to low, cover, and simmer for about 15 minutes, or until the water is absorbed and the quinoa is tender.
Remove from heat and let it sit, covered, for 5 minutes. Fluff with a fork and let it cool.
Prepare the Salad:
In a large mixing bowl, combine the black beans, red bell pepper, yellow bell pepper, red onion, cherry tomatoes, avocado, and cilantro.
Add the cumin, chili powder, and smoked paprika to the bowl and mix well.

Make the Dressing:
In a small bowl, whisk together the olive oil, lime juice, honey, minced garlic, salt, and black pepper until well combined.
Assemble the Salad:
Add the cooled quinoa to the salad mixture and toss gently to combine.
Pour the dressing over the salad and toss until everything is evenly coated.
Adjust seasoning to taste with additional salt, pepper, or lime juice if needed.
Serve:
Divide the salad among four plates or bowls.
Serve immediately or refrigerate for up to 2 days. This salad can be served chilled or at room temperature.

Nutritional Information (per serving):

Calories: 350
Total Fat: 14 grams
Saturated Fat: 2 grams

Sodium: 240 milligrams

Total Carbohydrates: 47 grams
Dietary Fiber: 12 grams

Chickpea and Veggie Buddha Bowl

Yield: 4 servings
Preparation Time: 20 minutes
Cooking Time: 25 minutes

Ingredients:

- **For the Roasted Chickpeas:**
- 1 can (400 grams) chickpeas, rinsed and drained
- 1 tablespoon olive oil (15 milliliters)
- 1 teaspoon smoked paprika
- 1/2 teaspoon ground cumin
- 1/2 teaspoon garlic powder
- 1/4 teaspoon salt
- 1/4 teaspoon black pepper
- **For the Vegetables:**
- 1 medium sweet potato, diced (200 grams)
- 1 red bell pepper, diced (150 grams)
- 1 zucchini, diced (200 grams)
- 1 tablespoon olive oil (15 milliliters)
- 1/2 teaspoon salt
- 1/4 teaspoon black pepper
- **For the Quinoa:**

- 200 grams quinoa
- 480 milliliters water
- **For the Dressing:**
- 60 milliliters tahini
- 60 milliliters lemon juice (about 1 large lemon)
- 1 tablespoon maple syrup (20 grams)
- 1 clove garlic, minced
- 1/4 teaspoon salt
- 60 milliliters water (adjust for desired consistency)
- **Additional Toppings:**
- 100 grams baby spinach
- 1 avocado, sliced (150 grams)
- 15 grams fresh cilantro, chopped
- 1 tablespoon sesame seeds (10 grams)

Instructions:
Prepare the Roasted Chickpeas:
Preheat the oven to 200°C (400°F).
In a bowl, toss the rinsed chickpeas with olive oil, smoked paprika, cumin, garlic powder, salt, and black pepper.
Spread the chickpeas on a baking sheet and roast for 20-25 minutes, shaking the pan halfway through, until crispy.
Roast the Vegetables:
In another bowl, toss the diced sweet potato, red bell pepper, and zucchini with olive oil, salt, and black pepper.
Spread the vegetables on a baking sheet and roast in the preheated oven for 20-25 minutes, or until tender and slightly caramelized.
Cook the Quinoa:
Rinse the quinoa under cold water.
In a medium saucepan, combine quinoa and water. Bring to a boil over medium-high heat.

Reduce heat to low, cover, and simmer for about 15 minutes, or until the water is absorbed and the quinoa is tender.
Remove from heat and let it sit, covered, for 5 minutes. Fluff with a fork and let it cool.
Make the Dressing:
In a small bowl, whisk together tahini, lemon juice, maple syrup, minced garlic, salt, and water. Adjust the water to reach your desired dressing consistency.
Assemble the Buddha Bowls:
Divide the cooked quinoa among four bowls.
Top each bowl with an equal portion of roasted chickpeas, roasted vegetables, baby spinach, avocado slices, and chopped cilantro.
Drizzle the tahini dressing over each bowl and sprinkle with sesame seeds.
Serve:
Serve immediately and enjoy a nutritious and heart-healthy meal.

Nutritional Information (per serving):

Protein: 15 grams
Sodium: 500 milligrams
Total Carbohydrates: 60 grams
Sugars: 10 grams
Saturated Fat: 2.5 grams

Calories:450
Total Fat: 18 g
Dietary Fiber: 14 grams

Asian-Inspired Chicken Salad

Yield: 4 servings
Preparation Time: 20 minutes
Cooking Time: 15 minutes

Ingredients:

- For the Salad:
- 2 skinless, boneless chicken breasts (400 grams)
- 1 tablespoon olive oil (15 milliliters)
- 200 grams mixed greens (e.g., spinach, kale, arugula)
- 1 medium carrot, julienned (60 grams)
- 1 medium red bell pepper, thinly sliced (150 grams)
- 1 small cucumber, thinly sliced (100 grams)
- 2 green onions, chopped (20 grams)
- 1 tablespoon sesame seeds (10 grams)

- For the Dressing:
- 60 milliliters low-sodium soy sauce
- 30 milliliters rice vinegar
- 1 tablespoon honey (20 grams)
- 1 tablespoon sesame oil (15 milliliters)
- 1 teaspoon grated ginger (5 grams)
- 1 clove garlic, minced
- 1 teaspoon sriracha sauce (optional) (5 milliliters)
- 1 tablespoon water (15 milliliters)

Instructions:

Prepare the Chicken:
Preheat the grill or a grill pan over medium-high heat.
Brush the chicken breasts with olive oil and season with a pinch of salt and pepper.
Grill the chicken for about 6-7 minutes on each side, or until fully cooked and the internal temperature reaches 75°C (165°F).
Remove from heat and let the chicken rest for 5 minutes before slicing it thinly.

Prepare the Salad:
In a large bowl, combine the mixed greens, julienned carrot, sliced red bell pepper, sliced cucumber, and chopped green onions.
Toss the vegetables to mix well.

Make the Dressing:
In a small bowl, whisk together the low-sodium soy sauce, rice vinegar, honey, sesame oil, grated ginger, minced garlic, sriracha sauce (if using), and water until well combined.
Assemble the Salad:
Divide the mixed salad vegetables among four plates.
Top each salad with an equal portion of sliced grilled chicken.
Drizzle the dressing evenly over the salads.
Sprinkle each salad with sesame seeds.

Serve:
Serve immediately and enjoy a fresh, nutritious, and heart-healthy meal.

Nutritional Information (per serving):

Calories: 300
Total Fat: 14 grams
Saturated Fat: 2 grams
Sodium: 600 milligrams

Total Carbohydrates: 14 grams
Dietary Fiber: 4 grams
Sugars: 8 grams
Protein: 30 grams

Shrimp and Avocado Salad

Yield: 4 servings
Preparation Time: 15 minutes
Cooking Time: 10 minutes

Ingredients:

- For the Salad:
- 450 grams raw shrimp, peeled and deveined

- 1 tablespoon olive oil (15 millilitres)

- 200 grams mixed greens (e.g., spinach, arugula, romaine)
- 1 large avocado, diced (150 grams)
- 1 medium cucumber, diced (150 grams)
- 1 medium red bell pepper, diced (150 grams)
- 1 small red onion, thinly sliced (50 grams)
- 10 grams fresh cilantro, chopped
- 1 tablespoon chia seeds (10 grams)

Instructions:
Prepare the Shrimp:
Preheat a grill or grill pan over medium-high heat.
Toss the shrimp with one tablespoon of olive oil.
Grill the shrimp on each side for about 2-3 minutes until they are pink and opaque.
Remove from heat and set aside.
Prepare the Salad:
In a large bowl, combine the mixed greens, diced avocado, cucumber, red bell pepper, thinly sliced red onion, and chopped cilantro.
Gently toss to mix the ingredients.
Make the Dressing:

- **For the Dressing:**
- 60 milliliters fresh lime juice
- 30 milliliters olive oil
- 1 teaspoon honey (7 grams)
- 1 clove garlic, minced
- 1 teaspoon ground cumin (5 grams)
- 1/2 teaspoon salt (2.5 grams)
- 1/4 teaspoon black pepper (1 gram)

In a small bowl, whisk together the fresh lime juice, olive oil, honey, minced garlic, ground cumin, salt, and black pepper until well combined.
Assemble the Salad:
Divide the salad mixture among four plates.
Top each salad with an equal portion of grilled shrimp.
Drizzle the dressing evenly over the salads.
Sprinkle each salad with chia seeds.
Serve:
Serve immediately and enjoy a fresh, nutritious, and heart-healthy meal.

Nutritional Information (per serving)

Calories: 320
Total Fat: 20 grams
Saturated Fat: 3 grams
Sodium: 430 milligrams

Total Carbohydrates: 14 grams
Dietary Fiber: 7 grams
Sugars: 4 grams
Protein: 22 grams

Curried Chickpea Salad

Yield: 4 servings
Preparation Time: 20 minutes
Cooking Time: 0 minutes (no cooking required)

Ingredients

- For the Salad:
- 400 grams canned chickpeas, drained and rinsed
- 150 grams cherry tomatoes, halved
- 1 medium cucumber, diced (150 grams)
- 1 medium red bell pepper, diced (150 grams)
- 1 small red onion, finely chopped (50 grams)
- 50 grams fresh spinach, chopped
- 30 grams fresh cilantro, chopped
- For the Dressing:

- 60 millilitres olive oil
- 30 millilitres lemon juice (juice of 1 lemon)
- 1 teaspoon ground cumin (5 grams)
- 1 teaspoon ground turmeric (5 grams)
- 1 teaspoon ground curry powder (5 grams)
- 1 teaspoon honey (7 grams)
- 1 clove garlic, minced
- 1/2 teaspoon salt (2.5 grams)
- 1/4 teaspoon black pepper (1 gram)

Instructions:
Prepare the Salad:
In a large bowl, combine the drained and rinsed chickpeas, halved cherry tomatoes, diced cucumber, diced red bell pepper, finely chopped red onion, chopped spinach, and chopped cilantro.
Gently toss the ingredients to mix them well.

Make the Dressing:
In a small bowl, whisk together the olive oil, lemon juice, ground cumin, ground turmeric, ground curry powder, honey, minced garlic, salt, and black pepper until well combined.
Assemble the Salad:

Pour the dressing over the salad mixture.
Toss gently to ensure all ingredients are well coated with the dressing.
Serve:

Divide the salad among four plates.
Serve immediately or refrigerate for 15-20 minutes to allow the flavors to meld together.

Nutritional Information (per serving):

Calories: 250
Total Fat: 14 grams
Saturated Fat: 2 grams
Sodium: 300 milligrams

Total Carbohydrates: 28 grams
Dietary Fiber: 8 grams
Sugars: 6 grams
Protein: 7 grams

Edamame and Quinoa Salad

Yield: 4 servings
Preparation Time: 15 minutes
Cooking Time: 20 minutes

Ingredients:

- **For the Salad:**
- 150 grams quinoa (uncooked)
- 300 milliliters water
- 200 grams shelled edamame (cooked and cooled)
- 100 grams cherry tomatoes, halved
- 1 medium cucumber, diced (150 grams)
- 1 small red bell pepper, diced (150 grams)
- 1 medium carrot, grated (70 grams)
- 50 grams red onion, finely chopped

- 30 grams fresh cilantro, chopped
- **For the Dressing:**
- 60 milliliters olive oil
- 30 milliliters lime juice (juice of 1 lime)
- 1 tablespoon rice vinegar (15 milliliters)
- 1 tablespoon low-sodium soy sauce (15 milliliters)
- 1 teaspoon honey (7 grams)
- 1 clove garlic, minced
- 1/4 teaspoon ground black pepper (1 gram)

Instructions:
Cook the Quinoa:
Rinse the quinoa under cold water to remove any bitterness.
In a medium saucepan, combine the quinoa and water.
Bring to a boil over medium-high heat.
Reduce the heat to low, cover, and simmer for 15-20 minutes, or until the water is absorbed and the quinoa is tender.
Remove from heat and let it sit, covered, for 5 minutes.
Fluff with a fork and let it cool.
Prepare the Salad:
In a large mixing bowl, combine the cooked quinoa, cooked and cooled edamame, halved cherry tomatoes, diced cucumber, diced red bell pepper, grated carrot, finely chopped red onion, and chopped cilantro.

Gently toss the ingredients to mix them well.
Make the Dressing:
In a small bowl, whisk together the olive oil, lime juice, rice vinegar, low-sodium soy sauce, honey, minced garlic, and ground black pepper until well combined.
Assemble the Salad:
Pour the dressing over the salad mixture.
Toss gently to ensure all ingredients are well coated with the dressing.
Serve:
Divide the salad among four plates.
Serve immediately or refrigerate for 15-20 minutes to allow the flavors to meld together.

Nutritional Information (per serving):

Calories: 310
Total Fat: 15 grams
Saturated Fat: 2 grams Sodium: 210 milligrams
Total Carbohydrates: 34 grams

Dietary Fiber: 7 grams
Sugars: 7 grams
Protein: 12 grams

Homemade heart-healthy dressings:

Spinach and Strawberry Salad with Poppy Seed Dressing

Yield: 4 servings
Preparation Time: 15 minutes

Ingredients:

- For the Salad:
- 200 grams baby spinach leaves
- 200 grams strawberries, hulled and sliced
- 50 grams red onion, thinly sliced
- 30 grams slivered almonds, toasted
- 30 grams feta cheese, crumbled
- For the Poppy Seed Dressing:

- 60 milliliters olive oil
- 30 milliliters apple cider vinegar
- 1 tablespoon honey
- 1 tablespoon poppy seeds
- 1 teaspoon Dijon mustard
- Salt and pepper to taste

Instructions:
Prepare the Salad:
In a large salad bowl, combine the baby spinach leaves, sliced strawberries, thinly sliced red onion, toasted slivered almonds, and crumbled feta cheese.
Make the Poppy Seed Dressing:
In a small bowl, whisk together the olive oil, apple cider vinegar, honey, poppy seeds, Dijon mustard, salt, and pepper until well combined.
Dress the Salad:

Drizzle the poppy seed dressing over the salad ingredients.
Toss the Salad:
Gently toss the salad until all ingredients are evenly coated with the dressing.
Serve:
Divide the salad among four plates.
Serve immediately as a light and refreshing side dish or starter.

Nutritional Information (per serving):
Calories: 180
Total Fat: 14 grams
Saturated Fat: 2 grams
Sodium: 120 milligrams

Total Carbohydrates: 11 grams
Dietary Fiber: 3 grams
Sugars: 7 grams
Protein: 4 grams

Tuna Salad with Greek Yogurt Dressing

Yield: 4 servings
Preparation Time: 15 minutes

Ingredients:

- For the Tuna Salad:
- 200 grams canned tuna in water, drained
- 100 grams cucumber, diced
- 100 grams cherry tomatoes, halved
- 50 grams red onion, finely chopped
- 50 grams celery, finely chopped
- 2 tablespoons fresh parsley, chopped

- For the Greek Yogurt Dressing:
- 150 grams Greek yogurt
- 1 tablespoon lemon juice
- 1 tablespoon extra virgin olive oil
- 1 clove garlic, minced
- 1 teaspoon dried dill
- Salt and pepper to taste

Instructions:

Prepare the Tuna Salad:
In a large mixing bowl, combine the drained tuna, diced cucumber, halved cherry tomatoes, finely chopped red onion, finely chopped celery, and chopped parsley. Mix well to combine.

Make the Greek Yogurt Dressing:
In a small bowl, whisk together the Greek yogurt, lemon juice, extra virgin olive oil, minced garlic, dried dill, salt, and pepper until smooth and creamy.

Nutritional Information (per serving)
Calories: 150
Total Fat: 6 grams
Saturated Fat: 1 gram
Cholesterol: 20 milligrams
Sodium: 250 milligrams

Dress the Tuna Salad:
Pour the Greek yogurt dressing over the tuna salad mixture.
Toss the Salad:
Gently toss the salad until all ingredients are evenly coated with the dressing.
Serve:
Divide the tuna salad among four plates or bowls. Serve immediately as a light and nutritious meal.

Total Carbohydrates: 7 grams
Dietary Fiber: 1 gram
Sugars: 3 grams
Protein: 17 grams

Greek Salad with Lemon Vinaigrette

Yield: 4 servings
Preparation Time: 15 minutes

Ingredients:

- **For the Salad:**
- 200 grams cherry tomatoes, halved
- 1 cucumber, diced
- 1 red bell pepper, diced
- 100 grams red onion, thinly sliced
- 100 grams Kalamata olives, pitted
- 100 grams feta cheese, crumbled
- 50 grams fresh parsley, chopped

- 50 grams fresh oregano leaves
- **For the Lemon Vinaigrette:**
- 60 milliliters extra virgin olive oil
- 2 tablespoons lemon juice
- 1 teaspoon Dijon mustard
- 1 clove garlic, minced
- 1 teaspoon dried oregano
- Salt and pepper to taste

Instructions:
Prepare the Salad:
In a large mixing bowl, combine the halved cherry tomatoes, diced cucumber, diced red bell pepper, thinly sliced red onion, pitted Kalamata olives, crumbled feta cheese, chopped parsley, and fresh oregano leaves. Toss gently to mix.
Make the Lemon Vinaigrette:
In a small bowl, whisk together the extra virgin olive oil, lemon juice, Dijon mustard, minced garlic, dried oregano, salt, and pepper until well combined.

Nutritional Information (per serving):

Calories: 220
Total Fat: 18 grams
Saturated Fat: 5 grams
Cholesterol: 15 milligrams

Dress the Salad:
Pour the lemon vinaigrette over the salad mixture.
Toss the Salad:
Gently toss the salad until all ingredients are evenly coated with the dressing.
Serve:
Divide the Greek salad among four plates or bowls.

Sodium: 450 milligrams
Total Carbohydrates: 10 grams
Dietary Fiber: 3 grams
Sugars: 5 grams
Protein: 6 gr

Quick Soups and Stews

Vegetable-based soups are a fantastic option for a heart-healthy lunch. They are packed with nutrients, low in calories, and incredibly versatile. Here are a few delicious and easy-to-make vegetable-based soups that will keep you satisfied and energized throughout the day.

Lentil Soup with Kale and Carrots

Yield: 6 servings
Preparation Time: 15 minutes
Cooking Time: 40 minutes

Ingredients

- 200 grams dried lentils, rinsed and drained
- 1 tablespoon olive oil
- 1 onion, finely chopped
- 2 cloves garlic, minced
- 2 carrots, diced
- 4 cups vegetable broth
- 2 cups water
- 2 cups chopped kale leaves
- 1 teaspoon dried thyme
- 1 teaspoon ground cumin
- Salt and pepper to taste
- Fresh lemon juice for serving
- Fresh parsley for garnish

Instructions:

Prepare the Lentils:
Rinse the dried lentils under cold water in a fine-mesh sieve. Drain well and set aside.

Sauté the Aromatics:
In a large pot, heat the olive oil over medium heat. Add the chopped onion and cook until softened, about 3-4 minutes.
Add the minced garlic and diced carrots to the pot. Cook for another 2 minutes, stirring occasionally.

Cook the Soup:
Pour the vegetable broth and water into the pot with the sautéed vegetables.
Add the rinsed and drained lentils, chopped kale leaves, dried thyme, and ground cumin.

Season with salt and pepper to taste.
Bring the soup to a boil, then reduce the heat to low.
Cover and simmer for 30-35 minutes, or until the lentils are tender.

Adjust Seasoning:
Taste the soup and adjust the seasoning with additional salt and pepper if needed.

Serve:
Ladle the lentil soup into serving bowls.
Squeeze a fresh lemon wedge over each serving before serving.
Garnish with fresh parsley if desired.

Nutritional Information (per serving)
Calories: 180
Total Fat: 3 grams
Saturated Fat: 0.5 grams
Cholesterol: 0 milligrams
Sodium: 580 milligrams
Total Carbohydrates: 30 grams
Dietary Fiber: 10 grams
Sugars: 4 grams
Protein: 10 grams

Red Lentil and Carrot Soup

Yield: 4 servings
Preparation Time: 10 minutes
Cooking Time: 25 minutes

Ingredients:

- 200 grams red lentils, rinsed and drained
- 2 tablespoons olive oil
- 1 onion, diced
- 2 cloves garlic, minced
- 2 carrots, diced
- 1 celery stalk, diced
- 4 cups vegetable broth
- 2 cups water

- 1 teaspoon ground cumin
- 1 teaspoon ground turmeric
- 1/2 teaspoon ground coriander

- Salt and pepper to taste
- Fresh lemon juice for serving
- Fresh cilantro for garnish

Instructions:
Prepare the Lentils:
Rinse the red lentils under cold water in a fine-mesh sieve. Drain well and set aside.
Sauté the Aromatics:
In a large pot, heat the olive oil over medium heat. Add the diced onion and cook until softened, about 3-4 minutes.
Add the minced garlic, diced carrots, and diced celery to the pot. Cook for another 3-4 minutes, stirring occasionally.
Cook the Soup:
Pour the vegetable broth and water into the pot with the sautéed vegetables.
Add the rinsed and drained red lentils to the pot.
Stir in the ground cumin, ground turmeric, and ground coriander.
Season with salt and pepper to taste.

Bring the soup to a boil, then reduce the heat to low. Cover and simmer for 20-25 minutes, or until the lentils and vegetables are tender.
Blend the Soup (Optional):
For a smoother texture, use an immersion blender to puree the soup until smooth. Alternatively, transfer the soup in batches to a blender and blend until smooth. Be careful when blending hot liquids.
Adjust Seasoning:
Taste the soup and adjust the seasoning with additional salt and pepper if needed.
Serve:
Ladle the red lentil and carrot soup into serving bowls. Squeeze a fresh lemon wedge over each serving before serving.
Garnish with fresh cilantro if desired.

Nutritional Information (per serving)

Calories: 230
Total Fat: 7 grams
Saturated Fat: 1 gram
Cholesterol: 0 milligrams

Sodium: 580 milligrams
Total Carbohydrates: 32 grams
Dietary Fiber: 12 grams
Sugars: 5 grams
Protein: 11 grams

Lean meat and legume stews

Lean meat and legume stews are hearty, nutritious, and perfect for a satisfying lunch. Combining lean proteins with fiber-rich legumes, these stews offer a balanced meal that is both filling and delicious. Here are a few recipes to inspire your lunchtime menu:

Sweet Potato and Black Bean Chili

Yield: 6 servings
Preparation Time: 15 minutes
Cooking Time: 40 minutes

Ingredients:

- 500 grams sweet potatoes, peeled and diced
- 1 tablespoon olive oil
- 1 onion, diced
- 2 cloves garlic, minced
- 1 red bell pepper, diced
- 1 green bell pepper, diced
- 1 jalapeño pepper, seeded and diced (optional)
- 1 tablespoon chili powder
- 1 teaspoon ground cumin

- 1/2 teaspoon smoked paprika
- 1/4 teaspoon cayenne pepper (adjust to taste)
- 1 can (400 grams) black beans, drained and rinsed
- 1 can (400 grams) diced tomatoes
- 2 cups vegetable broth
- Salt and pepper to taste
- Fresh cilantro, chopped, for garnish
- Avocado slices, for garnish

- Lime wedges, for serving

Instructions:
Prepare the Sweet Potatoes:
Peel and dice the sweet potatoes into small cubes.
Sauté the Aromatics:
In a large pot or Dutch oven, heat the olive oil over medium heat. Add the diced onion and cook until translucent, about 3-4 minutes.
Add the minced garlic, diced red bell pepper, green bell pepper, and jalapeño pepper (if using). Sauté for another 2-3 minutes until the peppers begin to soften.
Add Spices and Sweet Potatoes:
Sprinkle the chili powder, ground cumin, smoked paprika, and cayenne pepper over the sautéed vegetables. Stir to coat the vegetables evenly with the spices.
Add the diced sweet potatoes to the pot and stir to combine with the spices and vegetables.

Cook the Chili:
Pour in the drained and rinsed black beans, diced tomatoes (with their juices), and vegetable broth.
Stir well to combine all the ingredients.
Bring the chili to a boil, then reduce the heat to low.
Cover and simmer for 25-30 minutes, or until the sweet potatoes are tender and the chili has thickened to your desired consistency.
Season with salt and pepper to taste.
Serve:
Ladle the sweet potato and black bean chili into serving bowls.
Garnish with fresh chopped cilantro and avocado slices. Serve with lime wedges on the side for squeezing over the chili.

Nutritional Information (per serving)

Calories: 250
Total Fat: 5 grams
Saturated Fat: 1 gram
Cholesterol: 0 milligrams

Sodium: 480 milligrams
Total Carbohydrates: 45 grams
Dietary Fiber: 12 grams
Sugars: 8 grams
Protein: 9 grams

Spicy Chicken and Brown Rice Bowl

Yield: 4 servings
Preparation Time: 15 minutes
Cooking Time: 30 minutes

Ingredients:

- 400 grams boneless, skinless chicken breast, cut into bite-sized pieces
- 200 grams brown rice
- 1 tablespoon olive oil
- 1 onion, diced
- 2 cloves garlic, minced
- 1 red bell pepper, diced
- 1 green bell pepper, diced
- 1 cup broccoli florets
- 1 teaspoon smoked paprika
- 1/2 teaspoon cayenne pepper
- 1/2 teaspoon ground cumin
- Salt and pepper to taste
- Fresh cilantro, chopped, for garnish
- Lime wedges, for serving

Instructions:
Cook the Brown Rice:
Rinse the brown rice under cold water until the water runs clear.
In a medium saucepan, bring 2 cups of water to a boil. Add the rinsed brown rice and reduce the heat to low. Cover and simmer for 20-25 minutes, or until the rice is tender and all the water has been absorbed. Remove from heat and let it sit covered for 5 minutes. Fluff the rice with a fork.
Prepare the Chicken:

In a bowl, combine the chicken pieces with the smoked paprika, cayenne pepper, ground cumin, salt, and pepper. Toss well to coat the chicken evenly with the spices.
Cook the Chicken:
Heat olive oil in a large skillet over medium-high heat. Add the seasoned chicken pieces and cook for 6-8 minutes, or until they are browned and cooked through. Remove the chicken from the skillet and set aside.
Sauté the Vegetables:
In the same skillet, add diced onion and minced garlic. Sauté for 2-3 minutes until fragrant.

Add diced red bell pepper, green bell pepper, and broccoli florets to the skillet. Sauté for another 4-5 minutes, or until the vegetables are tender-crisp.
Combine Chicken and Vegetables:
Return the cooked chicken to the skillet with the sautéed vegetables. Stir well to combine.
Assemble the Bowls:

Divide the cooked brown rice evenly among serving bowls.
Top each bowl with the spicy chicken and vegetable mixture.
Garnish and Serve:
Garnish with fresh chopped cilantro and serve with lime wedges on the side for squeezing over the bowls.

Nutritional Information (per serving):

Calories: 350
Total Fat: 8 grams
Saturated Fat: 1 gram
Cholesterol: 70 milligrams

Sodium: 200 milligrams
Total Carbohydrates: 40 grams
Dietary Fiber: 5 grams
Sugars: 3 grams
Protein: 30 grams

Hearty Sandwiches and Wraps

Whole grain sandwiches are a perfect option for a heart-healthy lunch. They offer a balance of complex carbohydrates, protein, and fiber, ensuring you stay full and energized throughout the day. Here are a few delicious and nutritious whole-grain sandwich recipes to try:

Tomato Basil and Mozzarella Sandwich

Yield: 2 servings
Preparation Time: 10 minutes
Cooking Time: 5 minutes

Ingredients:

- 4 slices whole grain bread
- 2 medium tomatoes, thinly sliced
- 125 grams fresh mozzarella cheese, sliced
- 1/4 cup fresh basil leaves
- 1 tablespoon balsamic vinegar
- 1 tablespoon extra virgin olive oil
- Salt and pepper to taste

Instructions:
Prepare the Ingredients:
Slice the tomatoes and fresh mozzarella cheese into thin slices.
Rinse the fresh basil leaves and pat them dry with a paper towel.
Assemble the Sandwich:
Lay out 4 slices of whole grain bread on a clean surface.
Place tomato slices on two of the bread slices.
Top the tomatoes with fresh mozzarella slices.
Add fresh basil leaves on top of the mozzarella slices.
Drizzle balsamic vinegar and extra virgin olive oil over the basil leaves.
Season with salt and pepper to taste.
Complete the Sandwich:

Place the remaining two slices of bread on top of each assembled sandwich to form sandwiches.
Grill or Toast the Sandwich:
Preheat a grill pan or sandwich press over medium heat.
Place the assembled sandwiches on the grill pan or sandwich press.
Grill or toast for 2-3 minutes on each side, or until the bread is golden brown and the cheese is melted.
Serve:
Remove the sandwiches from the grill pan or sandwich press.
Slice each sandwich in half diagonally.
Serve immediately.

Nutritional Information (per serving):

Calories: 350
Total Fat: 15 grams
Saturated Fat: 6 grams
Cholesterol: 25 milligrams
Sodium: 400 milligrams

Total Carbohydrates: 35 grams
Dietary Fiber: 6 grams
Sugars: 7 grams
Protein: 18 grams

Whole Wheat Pasta Primavera

Yield: 4 servings
Preparation Time: 10 minutes
Cooking Time: 15 minutes

Ingredients:

- 250 grams whole wheat pasta
- 1 tablespoon olive oil
- 2 cloves garlic, minced
- 1 small onion, diced
- 1 medium carrot, julienned
- 1 medium zucchini, sliced
- 1 cup cherry tomatoes, halved
- 1 cup broccoli florets
- 1/2 cup bell pepper, thinly sliced
- 1/4 teaspoon dried oregano
- 1/4 teaspoon dried basil
- Salt and pepper to taste
- 2 tablespoons grated Parmesan cheese (optional)

Instructions:
Cook the Whole Wheat Pasta:
Bring a large pot of salted water to a boil.
Add the whole wheat pasta to the boiling water and cook according to the package instructions until al dente.
Once cooked, drain the pasta and set aside.
Prepare the Vegetables:
Heat olive oil in a large skillet over medium heat.
Add minced garlic and diced onion to the skillet. Sauté for 2-3 minutes until softened and fragrant.
Add julienned carrots, sliced zucchini, cherry tomatoes, broccoli florets, and sliced bell pepper to the skillet.
Season with dried oregano, dried basil, salt, and pepper.
Cook the Vegetables:

Sauté the vegetables for 5-7 minutes until they are tender but still crisp.
Stir occasionally to ensure even cooking.
Combine Pasta and Vegetables:
Add the cooked whole wheat pasta to the skillet with the sautéed vegetables.
Toss everything together until the pasta and vegetables are well combined.
Serve:
Divide the whole wheat pasta primavera among serving plates.
If desired, sprinkle grated Parmesan cheese over the pasta before serving.

Nutritional Information (per serving)

Calories: 300
Total Fat: 5 grams
Saturated Fat: 1 gram
Cholesterol: 0 milligrams

Sodium: 150 milligrams
Total Carbohydrates: 55 grams
Dietary Fiber: 8 grams
Sugars: 6 grams
Protein: 12 grams

Zucchini Noodles with Pesto and Cherry Tomatoes

Yield: 4 servings
Preparation Time: 15 minutes
Cooking Time: 10 minutes

43

Ingredients:

- 4 medium zucchini
- 200 grams cherry tomatoes, halved
- 2 tablespoons olive oil
- **For the Pesto:**
- 2 cups fresh basil leaves
- 50 grams pine nuts
- 2 cloves garlic

- 2 cloves garlic, minced
- Salt and pepper to taste
- Grated Parmesan cheese for garnish (optional)
- 50 grams grated Parmesan cheese
- 1/4 cup extra virgin olive oil
- Salt and pepper to taste

Instructions:

Prepare the Zucchini Noodles:

Using a spiralizer, spiralize the zucchini into noodles. If you don't have a spiralizer, you can use a vegetable peeler to create long, thin strips resembling noodles. Set aside.

Make the Pesto:

In a food processor, combine the fresh basil leaves, pine nuts, garlic, and grated Parmesan cheese.
Pulse until the ingredients are finely chopped.
With the food processor running, slowly drizzle in the olive oil until the pesto reaches a smooth consistency.
Season with salt and pepper to taste. Set aside.

Cook the Cherry Tomatoes:

Heat 1 tablespoon of olive oil in a large skillet over medium heat.
Add the minced garlic and cook for 1 minute until fragrant.
Add the halved cherry tomatoes to the skillet and cook for 3-4 minutes until they start to soften.
Season with salt and pepper to taste.

Cook the Zucchini Noodles:

In another skillet, heat the remaining tablespoon of olive oil over medium heat.
Add the zucchini noodles to the skillet and toss gently for 2-3 minutes until they are heated through but still slightly crisp.
Be careful not to overcook the noodles, as they can become mushy.

Combine Everything:

Add the cooked cherry tomatoes to the skillet with the zucchini noodles.
Pour the prepared pesto over the noodles and tomatoes.
Toss everything together until the noodles and tomatoes are evenly coated with the pesto.

Serve:

Divide the zucchini noodles with pesto and cherry tomatoes among serving plates.
If desired, garnish with grated Parmesan cheese before serving.

Nutritional Information (per serving)

Calories: 200
Total Fat: 16 grams
Saturated Fat: 3 grams
Cholesterol: 5 milligrams

Sodium: 150 milligrams
Total Carbohydrates: 10 grams
Dietary Fiber: 3 grams
Sugars: 5 grams
Protein: 6 grams

Healthy wrap ideas

Healthy wraps are a versatile and convenient option for a heart-healthy lunch. They can be filled with a variety of nutritious ingredients, making them both delicious and satisfying. Here are a few healthy wrap ideas to inspire your lunchtime menu:

Grilled Chicken and Avocado Wrap

Yield: 4 servings
Preparation Time: 15 minutes
Cooking Time: 10 minutes

Ingredients:

- 400 grams boneless, skinless chicken breasts
- 2 avocados, sliced
- 1 cup shredded lettuce
- 1 tomato, thinly sliced

- 1/2 red onion, thinly sliced
- 4 whole wheat tortillas
- **For the Marinade:**
- 2 tablespoons olive oil

- 2 cloves garlic, minced
- 1 teaspoon paprika
- 1 teaspoon ground cumin
- Salt and pepper to taste
- **For the Yogurt Sauce:**

- 1/2 cup Greek yogurt
- 1 tablespoon lemon juice
- 1 tablespoon chopped fresh cilantro
- Salt and pepper to taste

Instructions:
Marinate the Chicken:
In a bowl, whisk together olive oil, minced garlic, paprika, ground cumin, salt, and pepper to create the marinade.

Add the chicken breasts to the marinade, ensuring they are evenly coated.

Cover and refrigerate for at least 30 minutes to allow the flavors to meld.

Preheat the Grill:
Preheat a grill or grill pan over medium-high heat.

Grill the Chicken:
Remove the chicken breasts from the marinade and discard any excess marinade.

Grill the chicken for 5-6 minutes per side, or until cooked through and no longer pink in the center.

Remove from the grill and let rest for 5 minutes before slicing.

Prepare the Yogurt Sauce:

In a small bowl, combine Greek yogurt, lemon juice, chopped cilantro, salt, and pepper to make the yogurt sauce. Stir well to combine.

Assemble the Wraps:
Place a whole wheat tortilla on a clean work surface.

Spread a generous amount of yogurt sauce over the tortilla.

Layer shredded lettuce, sliced tomato, and red onion on top of the yogurt sauce.

Place sliced grilled chicken and avocado slices down the center of the tortilla.

Fold in the sides of the tortilla, then roll it up tightly into a wrap.

Serve:
Cut the wraps in half diagonally.

Serve immediately, or wrap tightly in foil or parchment paper for an on-the-go meal.

Nutritional Information (per serving):

Calories: 350
Total Fat: 15 grams
Saturated Fat: 2.5 grams
Cholesterol: 75 milligrams

Sodium: 300 milligrams
Total Carbohydrates: 25 grams
Dietary Fiber: 8 grams
Sugars: 3 grams
Protein: 30 grams

Turkey and Veggie Lettuce Wraps

Yield: 4 servings
Preparation Time: 20 minutes
Cooking Time: 10 minutes

Ingredients:

- 400 grams lean ground turkey
- 1 tablespoon olive oil
- 1 small onion, finely chopped
- 2 cloves garlic, minced
- 1 bell pepper, diced
- 1 carrot, grated
- 1 zucchini, grated

- 2 tablespoons low-sodium soy sauce
- 1 tablespoon hoisin sauce
- 1 teaspoon sesame oil
- Salt and pepper to taste
- 1 head iceberg or butter lettuce, leaves separated

Instructions:
Prepare the Turkey Mixture:
Heat olive oil in a large skillet over medium heat.

Add the chopped onion and minced garlic, sautéing until fragrant and translucent.

Add the ground turkey to the skillet, breaking it apart with a spatula, and cook until browned.

Add Vegetables:

Stir in the diced bell pepper, grated carrot, and grated zucchini.

Cook for an additional 3-4 minutes, until the vegetables are tender.

Season and Sauce:
Season the turkey and vegetable mixture with salt and pepper to taste.

Add low-sodium soy sauce, hoisin sauce, and sesame oil to the skillet.
Stir well to combine and cook for another 1-2 minutes.
Prepare Lettuce Wraps:
Wash and dry the lettuce leaves, then carefully separate them to create cups for the filling.

Spoon the turkey and vegetable mixture into the center of each lettuce leaf.
Serve:
Arrange the filled lettuce wraps on a serving platter.
Serve immediately, garnished with chopped green onions or sesame seeds if desired.

Nutritional Information (per serving):
Calories: 220
Total Fat: 10 grams
Saturated Fat: 2 grams
Cholesterol: 60 milligrams
Sodium: 350 milligrams

Total Carbohydrates: 8 grams
Dietary Fiber: 2 grams
Sugars: 4 grams
Protein: 25 grams

Mediterranean Hummus and Veggie Wrap

Yield: 4 servings
Preparation Time: 15 minutes

Ingredients:

- 4 whole wheat wraps or tortillas
- 200 grams hummus (store-bought or homemade)
- 1 large cucumber, thinly sliced
- 1 large tomato, thinly sliced
- 1 bell pepper, thinly sliced
- 1/2 red onion, thinly sliced
- 50 grams feta cheese, crumbled
- 1/4 cup Kalamata olives, pitted and chopped
- Fresh basil leaves, for garnish (optional)

Instructions:
Prepare the Ingredients:
Wash and prepare all the vegetables. Thinly slice the cucumber, tomato, bell pepper, and red onion. Crumble the feta cheese. Pit and chop the Kalamata olives.
Warm the Wraps:
If desired, warm the whole wheat wraps or tortillas in a microwave or skillet for a few seconds to make them more pliable.
Spread Hummus:
Lay out each wrap on a clean work surface.
Spread an even layer of hummus over the surface of each wrap, leaving a small border around the edges.
Layer the Vegetables:

Arrange the sliced cucumber, tomato, bell pepper, and red onion evenly over the hummus layer on each wrap.
Add Cheese and Olives:
Sprinkle crumbled feta cheese and chopped Kalamata olives over the vegetables on each wrap.
Roll the Wraps:
Starting from one end, tightly roll up each wrap, folding in the sides as you go to enclose the filling.
Serve or Store:
Slice the wraps in half diagonally, if desired, and garnish with fresh basil leaves.
Serve immediately, or wrap tightly in parchment paper or foil for a portable lunch option.

Nutritional Information (per serving)
Calories: 320
Total Fat: 14 grams
Saturated Fat: 3 grams
Cholesterol: 8 milligrams

Sodium: 650 milligrams
Total Carbohydrates: 40 grams
Dietary Fiber: 8 grams
Sugars: 5 grams
Protein: 12 gram

Barley and Vegetable Stir-Fry

Yield: 4 servings
Preparation Time: 10 minutes
Cooking Time: 20 minutes

Ingredients:

- 200 grams barley
- 2 tablespoons olive oil
- 2 cloves garlic, minced
- 1 onion, thinly sliced
- 2 carrots, julienned
- 1 bell pepper, thinly sliced
- 1 cup broccoli florets
- 1 cup snap peas
- 1 cup sliced mushrooms

- 2 tablespoons low-sodium soy sauce
- 1 tablespoon rice vinegar
- 1 tablespoon honey or maple syrup
- 1 teaspoon grated fresh ginger
- 1/2 teaspoon red pepper flakes (optional)
- Salt and pepper to taste
- Sesame seeds for garnish (optional)
- Fresh cilantro or green onions for garnish (optional)

Instructions:

Cook the Barley:
Rinse the barley under cold water. In a saucepan, bring 4 cups of water to a boil. Add the barley and reduce heat to low. Simmer, covered, for 20-25 minutes or until barley is tender. Drain any excess water and set aside.

Prepare the Stir-Fry Sauce:
In a small bowl, whisk together the soy sauce, rice vinegar, honey or maple syrup, grated ginger, and red pepper flakes (if using). Set aside.

Stir-Fry the Vegetables:
Heat the olive oil in a large skillet or wok over medium-high heat. Add the minced garlic and sliced onion, and cook for 1-2 minutes until fragrant.
Add the julienned carrots, sliced bell pepper, broccoli florets, snap peas, and sliced mushrooms to the skillet.

Stir-fry for 5-7 minutes until the vegetables are tender-crisp.

Combine with Barley:
Add the cooked barley to the skillet with the vegetables. Pour the prepared stir-fry sauce over the barley and vegetables. Stir well to combine and coat everything evenly with the sauce.

Finish and Serve:
Cook for an additional 2-3 minutes until everything is heated through and the sauce has thickened slightly. Season with salt and pepper to taste. Remove from heat. Garnish with sesame seeds, fresh cilantro or green onions if desired.

Serve the barley and vegetable stir-fry hot as a nutritious and satisfying meal.

Nutritional Information (per serving)

Calories: 280
Total Fat: 7 grams
Saturated Fat: 1 gram
Cholesterol: 0 milligrams

Sodium: 320 milligrams
Total Carbohydrates: 48 grams
Dietary Fiber: 10 grams
Sugars: 7 grams
Protein: 8 grams

Dinner Recipes

Balanced Main Dishes

Proper nutrition is key to a healthy heart. Foods rich in fiber, omega-3 fatty acids, antioxidants, and low in saturated fats can lower cholesterol, reduce inflammation, and support overall cardiovascular health. Make each meal a step towards a stronger heart!

Lemon Herb Grilled Salmon

Yield: 4 servings
Preparation time: 10 minutes
Marinating time: 30 minutes
Cooking time: 10 minutes

Ingredients:

- 4 salmon fillets (about 150g each), skin-on
- 2 tablespoons olive oil
- 2 cloves garlic, minced
- 2 tablespoons fresh lemon juice
- Zest of 1 lemon
- 1 teaspoon chopped fresh thyme
- 1 teaspoon chopped fresh rosemary
- 1 teaspoon chopped fresh parsley
- Salt and pepper to taste
- Lemon wedges, for serving

Instructions:

Prepare the Marinade:
In a small bowl, whisk together the olive oil, minced garlic, lemon juice, lemon zest, chopped thyme, chopped rosemary, chopped parsley, salt, and pepper.

Marinate the Salmon:
Place the salmon fillets in a shallow dish or a resealable plastic bag.
Pour the marinade over the salmon, making sure each fillet is evenly coated.
Cover the dish or seal the bag, and refrigerate for at least 30 minutes to allow the salmon to marinate.

Preheat the Grill:
Preheat your grill to medium-high heat (about 200-220°C).

Grill the Salmon:
Remove the salmon from the marinade and discard any excess marinade.
Place the salmon fillets on the preheated grill, skin-side down.
Grill for about 4-5 minutes on each side, or until the salmon is cooked through and easily flakes with a fork. The internal temperature should reach 145°F (63°C).

Serve:
Once cooked, remove the salmon from the grill and transfer to a serving platter.
Serve immediately with lemon wedges on the side.

Nutritional Information (per serving):

Calories: 295 kcal
Protein: 33g
Fat: 16g
Saturated Fat: 2.5g
Monounsaturated Fat: 8g
Polyunsaturated Fat: 4g
Cholesterol: 80mg
Carbohydrates: 2g
Fiber: 0.5g
Sugars: 0.5g
Sodium: 70mg

Baked Chicken with Garlic and Rosemary

Yield: 4 servings
Preparation Time: 10 minutes
Cooking Time: 30 minutes

Ingredients:

- 4 boneless, skinless chicken breasts (about 150g each)
- 4 cloves garlic, minced
- 2 tablespoons fresh rosemary, chopped
- 2 tablespoons olive oil
- 1 tablespoon lemon juice
- Salt and black pepper to taste

Instructions:

Preheat the oven to 200°C (400°F).

In a small bowl, mix together the minced garlic, chopped rosemary, olive oil, lemon juice, salt, and black pepper.

Place the chicken breasts in a baking dish and pour the garlic-rosemary mixture over them, ensuring they are evenly coated.

Cover the baking dish with foil and bake in the preheated oven for 20 minutes.

Remove the foil and continue baking for an additional 10 minutes, or until the chicken is cooked through and no longer pink in the center.

Once cooked, remove the chicken from the oven and let it rest for a few minutes before serving.

Serve the baked chicken with your choice of steamed vegetables or a side salad.

Nutritional Information (per serving):

Calories: 250 kcal
Protein: 25g
Carbohydrates: 2g
Fat: 15g
Saturated Fat: 3g
Cholesterol: 80mg

Sodium: 100mg
Fiber: 1g

Balsamic Glazed Pork Tenderloin

Yield: 4 servings
Preparation Time: 10 minutes
Marinating Time: 1 hour
Cooking Time: 25 minutes

Ingredients:

- 500g pork tenderloin
- 2 cloves garlic, minced
- 60ml balsamic vinegar
- 30ml low-sodium soy sauce
- 15ml honey
- 10ml olive oil
- 5ml Dijon mustard
- Salt and black pepper to taste
- Fresh rosemary sprigs for garnish (optional)

Instructions:

In a small bowl, whisk together the minced garlic, balsamic vinegar, soy sauce, honey, olive oil, Dijon mustard, salt, and black pepper to make the marinade.

Place the pork tenderloin in a shallow dish and pour the marinade over it, ensuring it is evenly coated. Cover and refrigerate for at least 1 hour, or overnight for best results.

Preheat the oven to 200°C (400°F).

.

Remove the pork tenderloin from the marinade and place it on a baking sheet lined with parchment paper.

Bake in the preheated oven for 20-25 minutes, or until the internal temperature reaches 63°C (145°F), basting occasionally with the marinade.

Once cooked, remove the pork from the oven and let it rest for 5 minutes before slicing.

Serve the sliced pork tenderloin garnished with fresh rosemary sprigs, if desired

Nutritional Information (per serving):

Calories: 250 kcal
Protein: 25g
Carbohydrates: 8g
Fat: 10g

Saturated Fat: 2g
Cholesterol: 75mg
Sodium: 300mg
Fiber: 0.5g

Grilled Shrimp and Asparagus Skewers

Yield: 4 servings
Preparation Time: 20 minutes
Cooking Time: 8-10 minutes

Ingredients:

- 400g large shrimp, peeled and deveined
- 400g asparagus spears, tough ends trimmed
- 2 tablespoons olive oil
- 2 cloves garlic, minced
- 1 tablespoon lemon juice
- 1 teaspoon lemon zest
- 1 teaspoon dried oregano
- 1/2 teaspoon paprika
- Salt and black pepper to taste
- Wooden skewers, soaked in water for 30 minutes

Instructions:

Preheat the grill to medium-high heat.

In a small bowl, whisk together the olive oil, minced garlic, lemon juice, lemon zest, dried oregano, paprika, salt, and black pepper to make the marinade.

Thread the shrimp and asparagus alternately onto the soaked wooden skewers.

Brush the skewers with the marinade, ensuring they are evenly coated.

Place the skewers on the preheated grill and cook for 4-5 minutes on each side, or until the shrimp are pink and opaque and the asparagus is tender-crisp, basting occasionally with the remaining marinade.

Once cooked, remove the skewers from the grill and serve immediately.

Nutritional Information (per serving):
Calories: 180 kcal
Protein: 20g
Carbohydrates: 4g
Fat: 10g

Saturated Fat: 1.5g
Cholesterol: 160mg
Sodium: 250mg
Fiber: 2g

Herb-Crusted Cod with Lemon

Yield: 4 servings
Preparation Time: 15 minutes
Cooking Time: 15 minutes

Ingredients:

- 4 cod fillets (about 150g each)
- 2 tablespoons olive oil
- 2 cloves garlic, minced
- 1 tablespoon fresh parsley, finely chopped
- 1 tablespoon fresh dill, finely chopped
- 1 tablespoon fresh chives, finely chopped
- Zest of 1 lemon
- Salt and black pepper to taste
- Lemon wedges for serving

Instructions:

Preheat the oven to 200°C (400°F). Line a baking sheet with parchment paper.

Pat the cod fillets dry with paper towels and place them on the prepared baking sheet.

In a small bowl, mix together the olive oil, minced garlic, chopped parsley, dill, chives, and lemon zest to make the herb mixture.

Brush each cod fillet with the herb mixture, ensuring they are evenly coated.

Season the fillets with salt and black pepper to taste.

Bake in the preheated oven for 12-15 minutes, or until the cod is opaque and flakes easily with a fork.

Remove from the oven and let the cod rest for a few minutes before serving.

Serve the herb-crusted cod with lemon wedges on the side.
Nutritional Information (per serving

Calories: 200 kcal
Protein: 25g
Carbohydrates: 2g Fat: 10g
Saturated Fat: 1.5g

Cholesterol: 60mg
Sodium: 100mg
Fiber: 0.5g

Greek Chicken Souvlaki

Yield: 4 servings
Preparation Time: 20 minutes
Marinating Time: 1 hour
Cooking Time: 10 minutes

Ingredients:

- 500g boneless, skinless chicken breast, cut into bite-sized pieces
- 2 tablespoons olive oil
- 2 cloves garlic, minced
- 1 teaspoon dried oregano
- 1 teaspoon dried thyme
- Juice of 1 lemon
- Zest of 1 lemon
- Salt and black pepper to taste
- 1 red bell pepper, cut into chunks
- 1 yellow bell pepper, cut into chunks
- 1 red onion, cut into chunks
- 8 cherry tomatoes
- 8 wooden skewers, soaked in water for 30 minutes
- **For Serving:**
- Whole wheat pita bread
- Tzatziki sauce
- Chopped fresh parsley
- Lemon wedges

Instructions:
In a large bowl, combine the olive oil, minced garlic, dried oregano, dried thyme, lemon juice, lemon zest, salt, and black pepper.
Add the chicken pieces to the marinade and toss until evenly coated. Cover and refrigerate for at least 1 hour.
Preheat the grill to medium-high heat.
Thread the marinated chicken onto the soaked wooden skewers, alternating with chunks of bell peppers, red onion, and cherry tomatoes.

Grill the skewers for 8-10 minutes, turning occasionally, until the chicken is cooked through and the vegetables are tender and slightly charred.
Remove the skewers from the grill and let them rest for a few minutes.
Serve the Greek chicken souvlaki with whole wheat pita bread, tzatziki sauce, chopped fresh parsley, and lemon wedges on the side.

Nutritional Information (per serving, excluding serving accompaniments):

Calories: 250 kcal
Protein: 28g
Carbohydrates: 9g
Fat: 11g

Saturated Fat: 1.5g
Cholesterol: 70mg
Sodium: 90mg
Fiber: 2g

Plant-based main dishes

Quinoa Stuffed Bell Peppers

Yield: 4 servings
Preparation Time: 20 minutes
Cooking Time: 40 minutes

Ingredients:

- 4 large bell peppers, any color
- 1 cup quinoa, rinsed
- 2 cups vegetable broth
- 1 tablespoon olive oil
- 1 small onion, diced
- 2 cloves garlic, minced
- 1 medium zucchini, diced
- 1 medium carrot, grated
- 1 cup cherry tomatoes, halved
- 1 teaspoon dried oregano
- 1 teaspoon dried basil
- Salt and pepper to taste
- 1/4 cup chopped fresh parsley
- 1/4 cup grated Parmesan cheese (optional)

Instructions:

Preheat the oven to 375°F (190°C). Line a baking dish with parchment paper.

Cut the tops off the bell peppers and remove the seeds and membranes. Place them upright in the prepared baking dish.

In a medium saucepan, combine the quinoa and vegetable broth. Bring to a boil, then reduce the heat to low, cover, and simmer for 15-20 minutes, or until the quinoa is cooked and the liquid is absorbed.

In a large skillet, heat the olive oil over medium heat. Add the diced onion and cook until softened, about 3-4 minutes. Add the minced garlic and cook for an additional minute.

Add the diced zucchini and grated carrot to the skillet. Cook for 5 minutes, or until the vegetables are tender.

Stir in the halved cherry tomatoes, dried oregano, dried basil, cooked quinoa, salt, and pepper. Cook for another 2-3 minutes, allowing the flavors to meld together.

Remove the skillet from the heat and stir in the chopped fresh parsley. Adjust the seasoning if needed.

Spoon the quinoa mixture into the hollowed-out bell peppers, dividing it evenly among them. If desired, sprinkle grated Parmesan cheese on top of each stuffed pepper.

Cover the baking dish with aluminum foil and bake in the preheated oven for 25-30 minutes, or until the peppers are tender.

Remove from the oven and let cool for a few minutes before serving.

Nutritional Information (per serving):

Calories: 250 kcal
Protein: 8g
Carbohydrates: 40g
Fat: 6g

Saturated Fat: 1g
Cholesterol: 0mg
Sodium: 400mg
Fiber:

Vegetable Stir-Fry with Tofu

Yield: 4 servings
Preparation Time: 15 minutes
Cooking Time: 15 minutes

Ingredients:

- 200g firm tofu, cubed
- 2 tablespoons low-sodium soy sauce
- 1 tablespoon sesame oil
- 1 tablespoon cornstarch
- 1 tablespoon olive oil
- 2 cloves garlic, minced
- 1 small onion, thinly sliced
- 1 medium carrot, julienned
- 1 red bell pepper, thinly sliced
- 1 yellow bell pepper, thinly sliced
- 1 cup broccoli florets
- 1 cup snap peas
- 1 cup sliced mushrooms
- 2 cups cooked brown rice or quinoa, for serving
- Sesame seeds, for garnish
- Chopped green onions, for garnish

Instructions:

In a bowl, toss the cubed tofu with low-sodium soy sauce, sesame oil, and cornstarch until evenly coated. Set aside to marinate for 10 minutes.

Heat olive oil in a large skillet or wok over medium-high heat. Add minced garlic and sliced onion, and stir-fry for 1-2 minutes until fragrant.

Add marinated tofu to the skillet and cook for 5-6 minutes, stirring occasionally, until golden brown and crispy. Remove tofu from the skillet and set aside.
In the same skillet, add julienned carrot, sliced bell peppers, broccoli florets, snap peas, and sliced mushrooms. Stir-fry for 4-5 minutes until the vegetables are tender-crisp.

Return the cooked tofu to the skillet with the vegetables and toss to combine.
Serve the vegetable stir-fry over cooked brown rice or quinoa.
Garnish with sesame seeds and chopped green onions before serving.

Nutritional Information (per serving):

Calories: 250 kcal
Protein: 12g
Carbohydrates: 30g
Fat: 10g

Saturated Fat: 1.5g
Cholesterol: 0mg
Sodium: 300mg
Fiber: 6g

Chickpea and Spinach Curry

Yield: 4 servings
Preparation Time: 10 minutes
Cooking Time: 25 minutes

Ingredients:

- 1 tablespoon olive oil
- 1 onion, finely chopped
- 3 cloves garlic, minced
- 1 teaspoon fresh ginger, grated
- 1 teaspoon ground cumin
- 1 teaspoon ground coriander
- 1/2 teaspoon turmeric powder
- 1/2 teaspoon paprika
- 1/4 teaspoon cayenne pepper (optional)

- 1 can (400g) chickpeas, drained and rinsed
- 1 can (400g) diced tomatoes
- 200g fresh spinach leaves
- 1/2 cup low-sodium vegetable broth
- Salt and pepper to taste
- Fresh cilantro, chopped, for garnish
- Cooked brown rice or whole grain naan, for serving

Instructions:
Heat olive oil in a large skillet over medium heat. Add chopped onion and cook until translucent, about 3-4 minutes.
Add minced garlic and grated ginger to the skillet, and cook for another 1-2 minutes until fragrant.
Stir in ground cumin, ground coriander, turmeric powder, paprika, and cayenne pepper (if using). Cook for 1 minute, stirring constantly.
Add drained chickpeas and diced tomatoes to the skillet. Stir well to combine.

Pour in the low-sodium vegetable broth and bring the mixture to a simmer. Reduce heat to low and let it cook for 10 minutes, allowing the flavors to meld together.
Add fresh spinach leaves to the skillet, a handful at a time, stirring until wilted.
Season the curry with salt and pepper to taste. Adjust the spices if needed.
Serve the chickpea and spinach curry hot over cooked brown rice or with whole grain naan.
Garnish with chopped fresh cilantro before serving.

Nutritional Information (per serving):

Calories: 220 kcal
Protein: 9g
Carbohydrates: 30g
Fat: 7g Saturated Fat: 1g

Cholesterol: 0mg
Sodium: 380mg
Fiber: 8g

Cauliflower Fried Rice

Yield: 4 servings
Preparation Time: 15 minutes
Cooking Time: 10 minutes

Ingredients:

- 1 medium head cauliflower, grated (about 600g)
- 1 tablespoon olive oil
- 2 cloves garlic, minced
- 1 small onion, finely chopped
- 1 carrot, diced
- 1/2 cup green peas (fresh or frozen)
- 2 eggs, lightly beaten

- 2 tablespoons low-sodium soy sauce
- 1 teaspoon sesame oil
- 1/2 teaspoon ground ginger
- 2 green onions, thinly sliced
- Salt and pepper to taste
- Sesame seeds, for garnish (optional)

Instructions:

Grate the cauliflower using a box grater or food processor until it resembles rice grains. Set aside.
In a large skillet or wok, heat olive oil over medium heat. Add minced garlic and chopped onion, and sauté until softened, about 2-3 minutes.
Add diced carrot and green peas to the skillet, and cook for another 2-3 minutes until the vegetables are tender-crisp.
Push the vegetables to one side of the skillet, and pour the lightly beaten eggs into the empty space. Scramble the eggs until fully cooked, then mix with the vegetables.

Stir in the grated cauliflower, low-sodium soy sauce, sesame oil, and ground ginger. Cook for 3-4 minutes, stirring occasionally, until the cauliflower is tender but not mushy.
Add sliced green onions to the skillet, and season with salt and pepper to taste. Stir well to combine.
Remove the cauliflower fried rice from heat and transfer to serving plates.
Garnish with sesame seeds if desired, and serve hot.

Nutritional Information (per serving):

Calories: 120 kcal
Protein: 5g
Carbohydrates: 12g
Fat: 6g

Saturated Fat: 1g
Cholesterol: 82mg
Sodium: 340mg
Fiber: 4g

Vegan Butternut Squash Risotto

Yield: 4 servings
Preparation Time: 15 minutes
Cooking Time: 35 minutes

Ingredients:

- 1 small butternut squash, peeled, seeded, and diced (about 500g)
- 2 tablespoons olive oil
- 1 onion, finely chopped
- 2 cloves garlic, minced
- 1 1/2 cups Arborio rice (300g)

- 4 cups low-sodium vegetable broth (1 litre)
- 1/2 cup dry white wine (120ml)
- 1/4 teaspoon ground nutmeg
- Salt and pepper to taste
- Fresh parsley, chopped, for garnish
- Vegan parmesan cheese, for serving (optional)

Instructions:

Preheat the oven to 200°C (400°F). Place the diced butternut squash on a baking sheet, drizzle with 1 tablespoon of olive oil, and season with salt and pepper. Roast in the preheated oven for 20-25 minutes or until tender.

In a large skillet or saucepan, heat the remaining olive oil over medium heat. Add the chopped onion and minced garlic, and sauté until soft and translucent, about 3-4 minutes.
Add the Arborio rice to the skillet and cook, stirring constantly, for 1-2 minutes until the rice is lightly toasted.

Pour in the dry white wine and cook, stirring occasionally, until the wine is absorbed by the rice. Gradually add the low-sodium vegetable broth, about 1/2 cup at a time, stirring frequently and allowing each addition to be absorbed before adding more. Cook for about 20 minutes or until the rice is creamy and tender.

Stir in the roasted butternut squash and ground nutmeg. Season with salt and pepper to taste.
Remove the skillet from heat and let it sit for a few minutes to allow the flavors to meld together.
Serve the vegan butternut squash risotto garnished with chopped fresh parsley and vegan parmesan cheese if desired

Nutritional Information (per serving):

Calories: 350 kcal
Protein: 7g
Carbohydrates: 64g
Fat: 7g

Saturated Fat: 1g
Cholesterol: 0mg
Sodium: 490mg
Fiber: 5g

Healthy Sides and Vegetables

Spaghetti Squash with Marinara Sauce

Yield: 4 servings
Preparation Time: 10 minutes
Cooking Time: 50 minutes

Ingredients:

- 1 medium spaghetti squash (about 1 kg)
- 1 tablespoon olive oil
- 2 cloves garlic, minced
- 1 can (400g) low-sodium diced tomatoes
- 1 teaspoon dried oregano

- 1 teaspoon dried basil
- Salt and pepper to taste
- Fresh basil leaves, chopped, for garnish
- Vegan parmesan cheese, for serving (optional)

Instructions:
Preheat the oven to 200°C (400°F). Cut the spaghetti squash in half lengthwise and scoop out the seeds. Place the halves cut-side down on a baking sheet lined with parchment paper.
Bake the spaghetti squash in the preheated oven for 40-45 minutes or until tender when pierced with a fork. Remove from the oven and let it cool slightly.
While the spaghetti squash is baking, prepare the marinara sauce. Heat the olive oil in a saucepan over medium heat. Add the minced garlic and sauté for 1 minute until fragrant.

Pour in the diced tomatoes with their juices. Add the dried oregano and basil. Season with salt and pepper to taste. Bring the sauce to a simmer and let it cook for 10-15 minutes, stirring occasionally, until slightly thickened. Once the spaghetti squash is cool enough to handle, use a fork to scrape the flesh into strands. Divide the spaghetti squash strands among serving plates.
Top each serving of spaghetti squash with marinara sauce. Garnish with chopped fresh basil leaves and vegan parmesan cheese if desired.

Nutritional Information (per serving):

Calories: 110 kcal
Protein: 2g
Carbohydrates: 16g
Fat: 5g

Saturated Fat: 1g
Cholesterol: 0mg
Sodium: 190mg
Fiber: 4g

Low-fat grains and legumes

Sweet Potato and Black Bean Enchiladas

Yield: 4 servings
Preparation Time: 20 minutes
Cooking Time: 30 minutes

Ingredients:

- 4 medium-sized whole wheat tortillas
- 2 large sweet potatoes, peeled and diced (about 500g)
- 1 can (400g) black beans, drained and rinsed
- 1 red bell pepper, diced
- 1 small onion, diced
- 2 cloves garlic, minced
- 1 teaspoon ground cumin
- 1 teaspoon chili powder
- Salt and pepper to taste
- 1 cup (240ml) low-sodium vegetable broth
- 1 cup (240ml) enchilada sauce
- 1 cup (120g) shredded reduced-fat cheddar cheese
- Fresh cilantro leaves, chopped, for garnish

Instructions:

Preheat the oven to 180°C (350°F). Lightly grease a baking dish with olive oil or cooking spray.

Place the diced sweet potatoes in a microwave-safe bowl and microwave on high for 5-7 minutes, or until tender. Alternatively, you can steam or roast the sweet potatoes until tender.

In a large skillet, heat a small amount of olive oil over medium heat. Add the diced onion and cook until softened, about 3-4 minutes. Add the minced garlic and cook for an additional minute.

Stir in the diced bell pepper, cooked sweet potatoes, black beans, ground cumin, chili powder, salt, and pepper. Cook for another 2-3 minutes until the vegetables are well combined and heated through.

Warm the whole wheat tortillas in the microwave or on a skillet for a few seconds to make them pliable.

Spoon the sweet potato and black bean mixture evenly onto each tortilla. Roll up the tortillas and place them seam-side down in the prepared baking dish.

Pour the vegetable broth and enchilada sauce over the rolled tortillas, making sure they are evenly coated.

Sprinkle the shredded reduced-fat cheddar cheese over the top of the enchiladas.

Cover the baking dish with aluminum foil and bake in the preheated oven for 20 minutes. Remove the foil and bake for an additional 5-10 minutes, or until the cheese is melted and bubbly.

Garnish the enchiladas with chopped fresh cilantro leaves before serving.

Nutritional Information (per serving):

Calories: 380 kcal
Protein: 17g
Carbohydrates: 63g
Fat: 6g

Saturated Fat: 3g
Cholesterol: 10mg
Sodium: 600mg
Fiber: 14g

Roasted Vegetable and Quinoa Salad

Yield: 4 servings
Preparation Time: 20 minutes
Cooking Time: 40 minutes

Ingredients:

- 1 cup (170g) quinoa, rinsed
- 2 cups (480ml) low-sodium vegetable broth
- 1 medium zucchini, diced (200g)
- 1 red bell pepper, diced (150g)
- 1 yellow bell pepper, diced (150g)
- 1 medium red onion, diced (150g)
- 1 cup (150g) cherry tomatoes, halved
- 2 tablespoons (30ml) extra virgin olive oil
- 1 teaspoon dried oregano
- 1 teaspoon dried basil
- 1/2 teaspoon garlic powder
- 1/4 teaspoon salt
- 1/4 teaspoon black pepper
- 1/4 cup (15g) fresh parsley, chopped
- 1/4 cup (25g) feta cheese, crumbled (optional)
- Juice of 1 lemon (about 3 tablespoons, 45ml)

Instructions:

Preheat the oven to 200°C (400°F).

Rinse the quinoa thoroughly under cold water. In a medium saucepan, combine the quinoa and vegetable broth. Bring to a boil, then reduce heat to low, cover, and simmer for 15-20 minutes, or until the quinoa is cooked and the liquid is absorbed. Fluff with a fork and set aside to cool.

While the quinoa is cooking, prepare the vegetables. Place the diced zucchini, red bell pepper, yellow bell pepper, and red onion on a large baking sheet. Drizzle with 1 tablespoon of the olive oil and sprinkle with dried oregano, dried basil, garlic powder, salt, and black pepper. Toss to coat evenly.

Roast the vegetables in the preheated oven for 25-30 minutes, stirring halfway through, until they are tender and lightly browned.

In a large mixing bowl, combine the cooked quinoa, roasted vegetables, cherry tomatoes, chopped parsley, and crumbled feta cheese (if using).

In a small bowl, whisk together the remaining 1 tablespoon of olive oil and the lemon juice. Pour over the quinoa and vegetable mixture and toss to combine. Serve the salad warm or at room temperature.

Nutritional Information (per serving):

Calories: 280 kcal
Protein: 8g
Carbohydrates: 35g
Fat: 12g

Saturated Fat: 2g
Cholesterol: 5mg (optional feta)
Sodium: 180mg
Fiber: 7g

Stuffed Portobello Mushrooms

Yield: 4 servings
Preparation Time: 15 minutes
Cooking Time: 30 minutes

Ingredients:

- 4 large Portobello mushrooms (about 600g)
- 2 tablespoons (30ml) extra virgin olive oil
- 1 small onion, finely chopped (100g)
- 2 cloves garlic, minced
- 1 red bell pepper, diced (150g)
- 1 small zucchini, diced (200g)
- 1 cup (100g) fresh spinach, chopped
- 1/2 cup (90g) quinoa, cooked
- 1/4 cup (15g) breadcrumbs (whole wheat if possible)
- 1/4 cup (30g) grated Parmesan cheese (optional)
- 1 teaspoon dried oregano
- 1 teaspoon dried basil
- 1/4 teaspoon salt
- 1/4 teaspoon black pepper
- 1 tablespoon (15ml) balsamic vinegar
- 2 tablespoons (8g) fresh parsley, chopped

Instructions:

Preheat the oven to 200°C (400°F).

Clean the Portobello mushrooms and remove the stems. Use a spoon to gently scrape out the gills from the underside of the mushrooms. Brush the mushrooms with 1 tablespoon of olive oil and place them on a baking sheet, gill side up.

In a large skillet, heat the remaining 1 tablespoon of olive oil over medium heat. Add the chopped onion and garlic, and sauté for 2-3 minutes until softened.

Add the diced red bell pepper and zucchini to the skillet. Cook for 5-7 minutes, until the vegetables are tender.

Stir in the chopped spinach and cook for another 2 minutes until wilted.

Remove the skillet from heat and stir in the cooked quinoa, breadcrumbs, Parmesan cheese (if using), dried oregano, dried basil, salt, black pepper, balsamic vinegar, and chopped parsley. Mix well to combine.

Divide the vegetable-quinoa mixture evenly among the Portobello mushrooms, stuffing each cap generously.

Bake the stuffed mushrooms in the preheated oven for 20-25 minutes, until the mushrooms are tender and the filling is golden brown on top.

Serve warm, garnished with additional fresh parsley if desired.

Nutritional Information (per serving):

Calories: 200 kcal
Protein: 8g
Saturated Fat: 2g
Cholesterol: 5mg (optional Parmesan)

Carbohydrates: 23g
Fat: 10g
Sodium: 200mg
Fiber: 5g

Teriyaki Tofu and Broccoli Stir-Fry

Yield: 4 servings
Preparation Time: 20 minutes
Cooking Time: 15 minutes

Ingredients:

- 400g firm tofu, drained and pressed
- 1 tablespoon (15ml) extra virgin olive oil
- 1 medium onion, thinly sliced (100g)
- 2 cloves garlic, minced
- 1 tablespoon (15g) fresh ginger, grated
- 1 large head broccoli, cut into florets (300g)
- 1 red bell pepper, sliced (150g)
- 2 medium carrots, thinly sliced (150g)

- 2 tablespoons (30ml) low-sodium soy sauce
- 2 tablespoons (30ml) water
- 1 tablespoon (15ml) rice vinegar
- 1 tablespoon (15ml) honey or maple syrup
- 1 teaspoon (5ml) sesame oil
- 1 teaspoon (5g) cornstarch
- 2 tablespoons (16g) sesame seeds, toasted
- 2 green onions, chopped (30g)

Instructions:
Prepare Tofu: Cut the pressed tofu into 2.5 cm cubes. Pat dry with a paper towel.
Make Sauce: In a small bowl, whisk together the low-sodium soy sauce, water, rice vinegar, honey (or maple syrup), sesame oil, and cornstarch. Set aside.
Cook Tofu: Heat 1 tablespoon of extra virgin olive oil in a large non-stick skillet or wok over medium-high heat. Add the tofu cubes and cook until golden brown on all sides, about 5-7 minutes. Remove tofu from the skillet and set aside.
Cook Vegetables: In the same skillet, add the sliced onion and cook for 2 minutes until slightly softened. Add the minced garlic and grated ginger, and cook for another minute until fragrant.

Add Broccoli and Carrots: Add the broccoli florets and sliced carrots to the skillet, and stir-fry for 5 minutes until they begin to soften.
Add Bell Pepper: Add the sliced red bell pepper to the skillet and cook for an additional 3 minutes.
Combine Tofu and Sauce: Return the tofu to the skillet. Pour the prepared sauce over the tofu and vegetables, stirring to coat evenly. Cook for 2-3 minutes until the sauce thickens and the vegetables are tender but crisp.
Garnish: Remove from heat and sprinkle with toasted sesame seeds and chopped green onions.
Serve: Serve immediately over a bed of brown rice or quinoa for added fiber and nutrients.

Nutritional Information (per serving):

Calories: 200 kcal
Protein: 12g
Saturated Fat: 1g
Cholesterol: 0mg

Carbohydrates: 22g
Fat: 9g
Sodium: 300mg
Fiber: 6g

Comfort Food Made Healthy

Lentil and Mushroom Shepherd's Pie

Yield: 6 servings
Preparation Time: 20 minutes
Cooking Time: 50 minutes

Ingredients:

- For the filling:
- 1 tablespoon (15ml) extra virgin olive oil
- 1 large onion, finely chopped (150g)
- 2 cloves garlic, minced
- 2 medium carrots, diced (200g)
- 2 celery stalks, diced (100g)
- 250g mushrooms, sliced
- 200g dried green or brown lentils, rinsed and drained
- For the mashed potato topping:
- 1kg potatoes, peeled and chopped
- 1 tablespoon (15ml) extra virgin olive oil
- 1 tablespoon (15g) tomato paste
- 1 teaspoon (5g) ground cumin
- 1 teaspoon (5g) ground paprika
- 1/2 teaspoon (2.5g) ground black pepper
- 800ml low-sodium vegetable broth
- 1 tablespoon (15ml) balsamic vinegar
- 1 tablespoon (15g) fresh thyme leaves, chopped
- 100g frozen peas
- 120ml unsweetened almond milk (or other low-fat milk alternatives)
- 1/2 teaspoon (2.5g) ground black pepper
- 1/2 teaspoon (2.5g) garlic powder

Instructions:

Prepare the potatoes:

Place the chopped potatoes in a large pot and cover with water. Bring to a boil and cook for about 15 minutes, or until tender. Drain and return to the pot.

Add 1 tablespoon of olive oil, almond milk, black pepper, and garlic powder to the potatoes. Mash until smooth and set aside.

Prepare the filling:

Preheat your oven to 200°C (400°F).

In a large skillet, heat 1 tablespoon of olive oil over medium heat. Add the chopped onion and cook for 5 minutes until translucent.

Add the minced garlic, diced carrots, and celery. Cook for another 5 minutes until the vegetables begin to soften.

Add the sliced mushrooms and cook for another 5 minutes until they release their moisture and start to brown.

Stir in the rinsed lentils, tomato paste, ground cumin, ground paprika, and ground black pepper. Cook for 2 minutes.

Pour in the low-sodium vegetable broth and balsamic vinegar. Bring the mixture to a boil, then reduce heat and simmer for 20-25 minutes, or until the lentils are tender and most of the liquid has been absorbed.

Stir in the fresh thyme leaves and frozen peas. Cook for another 2 minutes, then remove from heat.

Assemble the Shepherd's Pie:

Transfer the lentil and mushroom filling to a large baking dish.

Spread the mashed potatoes evenly over the top of the filling, creating a smooth layer. Use a fork to create a decorative pattern on the mashed potatoes, if desired.

Bake:

Place the baking dish in the preheated oven and bake for 20 minutes, or until the top is golden brown and the filling is bubbling.

Serve:

Remove from the oven and let the shepherd's pie sit for a few minutes before serving.

Nutritional Information (per serving):

Calories: 280 kcal

Protein: 10g

Carbohydrates: 45g

Fat: 7g

Saturated Fat: 1g

Cholesterol: 0mg

Sodium: 200mg

Fiber: 10g

Turkey Meatloaf with Tomato Glaze

Yield: 6 servings
Preparation Time: 15 minutes
Cooking Time: 1 hour

Ingredients:

- **For the meatloaf:**
- 500g ground turkey (93% lean)
- 1 large onion, finely chopped (150g)
- 2 cloves garlic, minced
- 1 medium carrot, grated (70g)
- 1 celery stalk, finely chopped (50g)
- 50g rolled oats

- 1 large egg, lightly beaten
- 60ml unsweetened almond milk (or other low-fat milk alternatives)
- 2 tablespoons (30ml) Worcestershire sauce (low sodium)
- 1 tablespoon (15g) Dijon mustard
- **For the tomato glaze:**
- 120ml no-sugar-added ketchup

- 1 tablespoon (15g) tomato paste
- 1 teaspoon (5g) dried thyme
- 1 teaspoon (5g) dried oregano
- 1/2 teaspoon (2.5g) ground black pepper
- 1/2 teaspoon (2.5g) salt

- 1 tablespoon (15ml) balsamic vinegar
- 1 tablespoon (15g) brown sugar

Instructions:

Preheat the Oven:
Preheat your oven to 180°C (350°F). Line a baking sheet with parchment paper or lightly grease a loaf pan.
Prepare the Meatloaf Mixture:
In a large mixing bowl, combine the ground turkey, finely chopped onion, minced garlic, grated carrot, chopped celery, and rolled oats.
In a separate small bowl, whisk together the beaten egg, almond milk, Worcestershire sauce, Dijon mustard, tomato paste, dried thyme, dried oregano, ground black pepper, and salt.
Pour the wet mixture into the bowl with the turkey and vegetables. Mix everything until well combined but do not overmix to avoid a dense meatloaf.
Shape the Meatloaf:
Transfer the meatloaf mixture to the prepared baking sheet or loaf pan. Shape it into a loaf, smoothing the top with a spatula.

Prepare the Tomato Glaze:
In a small bowl, mix together the no-sugar-added ketchup, balsamic vinegar, and brown sugar until well combined.
Bake the Meatloaf:
Spread half of the tomato glaze evenly over the top of the meatloaf.
Place the meatloaf in the preheated oven and bake for 45 minutes.
Remove the meatloaf from the oven and spread the remaining tomato glaze over the top. Return to the oven and bake for an additional 15 minutes, or until the internal temperature reaches 75°C (165°F).
Rest and Serve:
Allow the meatloaf to rest for 10 minutes before slicing and serving.

Nutritional Information (per serving):

Calories: 220 kcal
Protein: 25g
Carbohydrates: 15g
Fat: 8g

Saturated Fat: 2g
Cholesterol: 85mg
Sodium: 360mg
Fiber: 2g

Moroccan-Spiced Chicken Thighs

Yield: 4 servings
Preparation Time: 20 minutes
Cooking Time: 40 minutes

Ingredients:

- 600g boneless, skinless chicken thighs
- 2 tablespoons (30ml) olive oil
- 1 large onion, finely chopped (150g)
- 3 cloves garlic, minced
- 1 teaspoon (5g) ground cumin
- 1 teaspoon (5g) ground coriander
- 1 teaspoon (5g) ground paprika
- 1/2 teaspoon (2.5g) ground cinnamon
- 1/2 teaspoon (2.5g) ground turmeric

- 1/4 teaspoon (1.25g) cayenne pepper (optional, for heat)
- 1 teaspoon (5g) ground black pepper
- 1/2 teaspoon (2.5g) salt
- 400g canned chickpeas, drained and rinsed
- 400g canned diced tomatoes (no salt added)
- 1 medium carrot, diced (70g)
- 1 medium zucchini, diced (120g)
- 120ml low-sodium chicken broth

- 2 tablespoons (30ml) lemon juice

- Fresh cilantro for garnish

Instructions:
Prepare the Chicken:
In a small bowl, mix together the ground cumin, ground coriander, ground paprika, ground cinnamon, ground turmeric, cayenne pepper (if using), ground black pepper, and salt.
Rub the spice mixture evenly over the chicken thighs.
Sear the Chicken:
Heat 1 tablespoon (15ml) of olive oil in a large, deep skillet over medium-high heat. Add the chicken thighs and sear for 3-4 minutes on each side, until browned. Remove the chicken from the skillet and set aside.
Sauté the Aromatics:
In the same skillet, add the remaining 1 tablespoon (15ml) of olive oil. Add the finely chopped onion and cook for 5 minutes until translucent. Add the minced garlic and cook for an additional minute.

Add Vegetables and Chickpeas:
Add the diced carrot and diced zucchini to the skillet. Cook for 5 minutes, stirring occasionally, until they begin to soften. Add the canned chickpeas and diced tomatoes, stirring to combine.
Simmer with Chicken:
Return the seared chicken thighs to the skillet. Add the low-sodium chicken broth and bring to a simmer. Cover the skillet, reduce the heat to low, and let it simmer for 20-25 minutes, or until the chicken is cooked through and the vegetables are tender.
Finish and Serve:
Stir in the lemon juice. Taste and adjust seasoning if necessary.
Garnish with fresh cilantro before serving.

Nutritional Information (per serving):

Calories: 320 kcal
Protein: 28g
Carbohydrates: 20g Fat: 14g
Saturated Fat: 2g

Cholesterol: 110mg
Sodium: 420mg
Fiber: 5g

Barley and Vegetable Soup

Yield: 6 servings
Preparation Time: 15 minutes
Cooking Time: 45 minutes

Ingredients:

- 1 tablespoon (15ml) olive oil
- 1 large onion, finely chopped (150g)
- 2 cloves garlic, minced
- 2 medium carrots, diced (140g)
- 2 celery stalks, diced (120g)
- 1 large zucchini, diced (200g)
- 1 red bell pepper, diced (150g)
- 150g pearl barley, rinsed
- 1 can (400g) diced tomatoes (no salt added)

- 1.2 liters low-sodium vegetable broth
- 1 teaspoon (5g) dried thyme
- 1 teaspoon (5g) dried oregano
- 1 bay leaf
- 1 teaspoon (5g) ground black pepper
- 1/2 teaspoon (2.5g) salt (optional)
- 150g kale, chopped (remove tough stems)
- Juice of 1 lemon (30ml)
- Fresh parsley, chopped, for garnish

Instructions:
Prepare the Vegetables:
Dice the onion, carrots, celery, zucchini, and red bell pepper. Mince the garlic and chop the kale, removing the tough stems.
Sauté the Aromatics:

In a large pot, heat the olive oil over medium heat. Add the finely chopped onion and cook for about 5 minutes until translucent. Add the minced garlic and cook for an additional minute.
Add Vegetables and Barley:

Add the diced carrots, celery, zucchini, and red bell pepper to the pot. Cook for 5 minutes, stirring occasionally. Add the rinsed barley and stir to combine.

Add Liquids and Seasonings:

Pour in the diced tomatoes and low-sodium vegetable broth. Stir in the dried thyme, dried oregano, bay leaf, ground black pepper, and salt (if using). Bring the mixture to a boil.

Simmer the Soup:

Reduce the heat to low, cover the pot, and let the soup simmer for 30 minutes, or until the barley is tender and the vegetables are cooked through.

Add Kale and Lemon Juice:

Stir in the chopped kale and lemon juice. Cook for an additional 5 minutes until the kale is wilted.

Serve:

Remove the bay leaf. Ladle the soup into bowls and garnish with fresh parsley.

Nutritional Information (per serving):

Calories: 190 kcal
Protein: 5g
Carbohydrates: 32g
Fat: 4g

Saturated Fat: 0.5g
Cholesterol: 0mg
Sodium: 150mg
Fiber: 8g.

Snacks and Appetizers

Quick and Healthy Snack Ideas

Mixed Nuts and Dried Fruit Mix

Yield: 8 servings
Preparation Time: 10 minutes
Ingredients:

- 100 grams almonds (unsalted, raw)
- 100 grams walnuts (unsalted, raw)
- 100 grams cashews (unsalted, raw)
- 50 grams pecans (unsalted, raw)
- 50 grams pumpkin seeds (unsalted, raw)
- 50 grams sunflower seeds (unsalted, raw)
- 75 grams dried cranberries (unsweetened)
- 75 grams dried apricots (unsweetened, chopped)
- 50 grams raisins (unsweetened)
- 50 grams dried blueberries (unsweetened)

Instructions:
Preparation: Measure all ingredients accurately using a kitchen scale for precise quantities.
Mixing: In a large mixing bowl, combine the almonds, walnuts, cashews, pecans, pumpkin seeds, and sunflower seeds.
Adding Dried Fruits: Add the dried cranberries, chopped dried apricots, raisins, and dried blueberries to the nut mixture.

Tossing: Gently toss all ingredients together until well mixed.
Serving: Divide the mix into 8 equal portions. Store in airtight containers or zip-lock bags for easy access and to maintain freshness.

Nutritional Information (per serving):

Calories: 250 kcal
Total Fat: 18 grams
Saturated Fat: 2 grams
Monounsaturated Fat: 8 grams
Polyunsaturated Fat: 5 grams
Fat: 4g

Saturated Fat: 0.5g
Cholesterol: 0mg
Sodium: 150mg
Fiber:10g

Roasted Chickpeas with Spices

Yield: 4 servings
Preparation Time: 5 minutes
Cooking Time: 40 minutes

Ingredients:

- 400 grams canned chickpeas (drained and rinsed)
- 2 tablespoons olive oil
- 1 teaspoon smoked paprika
- 1 teaspoon garlic powder
- 1/2 teaspoon ground cumin
- 1/2 teaspoon ground coriander
- 1/4 teaspoon cayenne pepper (optional)
- Salt to taste

Instructions:
Preheat Oven: Preheat your oven to 200°C (400°F).
Dry Chickpeas: Pat the rinsed chickpeas dry with a paper towel or kitchen towel to remove excess moisture.
Seasoning: In a mixing bowl, combine the chickpeas with olive oil, smoked paprika, garlic powder, ground cumin, ground coriander, cayenne pepper (if using), and salt.

Toss until the chickpeas are evenly coated with the spices.
Baking: Spread the seasoned chickpeas in a single layer on a baking sheet lined with parchment paper.

Roasting: Roast in the preheated oven for 30-40 minutes, stirring halfway through, until the chickpeas are crispy and golden brown.

Cooling: Allow the roasted chickpeas to cool for a few minutes before serving.

Nutritional Information (per serving):

Calories: 215 kcal
Total Fat: 9 grams
Saturated Fat: 1 gram
Monounsaturated Fat: 6 grams
Polyunsaturated Fat: 1.5 grams Cholesterol: 0 mg

Sodium: 320 mg
Total Carbohydrates: 26 grams
Dietary Fiber: 7 grams
Sugars: 1 gram
Protein: 8 grams

Veggie sticks and dips

Hummus and Veggie Platter

Yield: 4 servings
Preparation Time: 10 minutes
Cooking Time: 0 minutes

Ingredients:

- 400 grams canned chickpeas, drained and rinsed
- 2 tablespoons tahini
- 2 tablespoons lemon juice
- 2 cloves garlic, minced
- 1/2 teaspoon ground cumin
- 1/4 teaspoon paprika
- 1/4 teaspoon salt
- 60 milliliters water (adjust for desired consistency)
- Assorted fresh vegetables (carrots, cucumbers, bell peppers, cherry tomatoes, etc.), washed and sliced

Instructions:
Prepare the Hummus: In a food processor, combine the chickpeas, tahini, lemon juice, minced garlic, ground cumin, paprika, and salt.
Blend: Process the mixture until smooth, gradually adding water until you reach your desired consistency.
Adjust Seasoning: Taste the hummus and adjust the seasoning as needed, adding more lemon juice or salt if desired.

Prepare Vegetables: Wash and slice the assorted fresh vegetables into bite-sized pieces.
Serve: Transfer the hummus to a serving bowl and arrange the sliced vegetables around it on a platter.
Garnish: Optionally, drizzle a little olive oil over the hummus and sprinkle some extra paprika or chopped fresh herbs for garnish.
Enjoy: Serve immediately as a delicious and heart-healthy snack or appetizer.

Nutritional Information (per serving):

Calories: 165 kcal
Total Fat: 7 grams
Saturated Fat: 1 gram
Polyunsaturated Fat: 2 grams
Monounsaturated Fat: 4 grams
Cholesterol: 0 mg

Sodium: 220 mg
Total Carbohydrates: 21 grams
Dietary Fiber: 6 grams
Sugars: 2 grams
Protein: 7 grams

Roasted Red Pepper and Walnut Dip

Yield: 6 servings

Preparation Time: 10 minutes
Cooking Time: 25 minutes

Ingredients:

- 2 large red bell peppers (about 400 grams)
- 50 grams walnuts
- 2 cloves garlic, minced
- 1 tablespoon lemon juice
- 1 tablespoon olive oil
- 1/2 teaspoon smoked paprika
- Salt and pepper to taste
- Fresh parsley or chives for garnish (optional)

Instructions:
Preheat the Oven: Preheat your oven to 200°C (400°F). Roast the Red Peppers: Cut the red peppers in half lengthwise and remove the seeds and membranes. Place them on a baking sheet, skin side up. Roast in the preheated oven for 20-25 minutes, or until the skins are charred and blistered.
Steam and Peel: Transfer the roasted red peppers to a bowl and cover with plastic wrap or a kitchen towel. Let them steam for about 10 minutes. Once cooled, peel off the skins and discard.

Prepare the Dip: In a food processor, combine the roasted red peppers, walnuts, minced garlic, lemon juice, olive oil, and smoked paprika. Blend until smooth and creamy. Season with salt and pepper to taste.
Adjust Consistency: If the dip is too thick, you can add a tablespoon of water at a time until you reach your desired consistency.
Garnish and Serve: Transfer the dip to a serving bowl and garnish with fresh parsley or chives if desired. Serve with sliced vegetables, whole grain crackers, or pita bread.

Nutritional Information (per serving):

Calories: 90 kcal
Total Fat: 8 grams
Saturated Fat: 1 gram
Polyunsaturated Fat: 5 grams
Monounsaturated Fat: 2 grams
Cholesterol: 0 mg

Sodium: 80 mg
Total Carbohydrates: 4 grams
Dietary Fiber: 1 gram
Sugars: 2 grams
Protein: 2 grams

Spicy Black Bean Dip with Veggie Sticks

Yield: 6 servings
Preparation Time: 10 minutes
Cooking Time: 5 minutes

Ingredients:

- 1 can (400 grams) black beans, drained and rinsed
- 1 tablespoon olive oil
- 1 small onion, diced
- 2 cloves garlic, minced
- 1 teaspoon ground cumin
- 1/2 teaspoon chili powder
- 1/4 teaspoon cayenne pepper (adjust to taste)
- 2 tablespoons fresh lime juice
- Salt and pepper to taste
- Assorted vegetables for serving (carrot sticks, cucumber slices, bell pepper strips, etc.)

Instructions:
Prepare the Black Beans: In a small saucepan, heat the olive oil over medium heat. Add the diced onion and minced garlic, and sauté until softened, about 3-4 minutes.

Add Spices: Add the ground cumin, chili powder, and cayenne pepper to the saucepan. Stir well and cook for another minute until fragrant.
Blend Ingredients: Transfer the sautéed onion and garlic mixture to a food processor. Add the drained black beans and fresh lime juice. Blend until smooth and

creamy. If the mixture is too thick, you can add a tablespoon of water to thin it out.

Season to Taste: Taste the dip and season with salt and pepper according to your preference. Adjust the amount of cayenne pepper for desired spiciness.

Serve with Veggie Sticks: Transfer the spicy black bean dip to a serving bowl. Arrange assorted vegetable sticks around the bowl for dipping.

Nutritional Information (per serving):

Calories: 90 kcal
Total Fat: 3 grams
Saturated Fat: 0.4 grams
Polyunsaturated Fat: 0.7 grams
Monounsaturated Fat: 1.8 grams
Cholesterol: 0 mg

Sodium: 150 mg
Total Carbohydrates: 14 grams
Dietary Fiber: 5 grams
Sugars: 2 grams
Protein: 4 grams

Whole Wheat Pita Chips and Guacamole

Yield: 4 servings
Preparation Time: 15 minutes
Cooking Time: 10 minutes

Ingredients:

- For Whole Wheat Pita Chips:
- 2 whole wheat pita bread rounds
- 1 tablespoon olive oil
- 1/2 teaspoon garlic powder
- 1/2 teaspoon paprika
- Salt to taste
- For Guacamole:

- 2 ripe avocados
- 1 small tomato, diced
- 1/4 cup red onion, finely chopped
- 1 clove garlic, minced
- 1 tablespoon fresh lime juice
- 2 tablespoons fresh cilantro, chopped
- Salt and pepper to taste

Instructions:
Preheat Oven: Preheat the oven to 375°F (190°C).
Prepare Pita Chips:
Cut each pita bread round into 8 wedges.
In a small bowl, mix olive oil, garlic powder, paprika, and salt.
Brush both sides of each pita wedge with the olive oil mixture.
Place the wedges on a baking sheet in a single layer.
Bake Pita Chips: Bake in the preheated oven for 8-10 minutes, or until the pita chips are golden brown and crispy. Remove from the oven and let cool.

Prepare Guacamole:
Cut the avocados in half and remove the pits. Scoop the avocado flesh into a medium bowl.
Mash the avocado with a fork until smooth or to your desired consistency.
Add diced tomato, chopped red onion, minced garlic, lime juice, and chopped cilantro to the bowl.
Season with salt and pepper to taste. Mix well to combine.
Serve: Transfer the guacamole to a serving bowl and serve with the whole wheat pita chips.

Nutritional Information (per serving):

Whole Wheat Pita Chips:
Calories: 120 kcal
Total Fat: 4 grams
Sodium: 160 mg
Total Carbohydrates: 18 grams
Dietary Fiber: 3 grams
Protein: 3 grams

Guacamole:
Calories: 150 kcal
Total Fat: 13 grams
Sodium: 10 mg
Total Carbohydrates: 9 grams
Dietary Fiber: 7 grams
Protein: 2 grams

Edamame Hummus

Yield: Approximately 2 cups
Preparation Time: 10 minutes
Cooking Time: 5 minutes

Ingredients:

- 300 grams shelled edamame (cooked and cooled)
- 2 tablespoons tahini
- 2 cloves garlic, minced
- 3 tablespoons fresh lemon juice
- 2 tablespoons extra virgin olive oil
- 1/2 teaspoon ground cumin
- 1/4 teaspoon smoked paprika
- Salt and pepper to taste
- 2-4 tablespoons water (as needed for desired consistency)

Instructions:

Prepare Edamame: If using frozen edamame, cook according to package instructions. Drain and rinse under cold water to cool.

Blend Ingredients: In a food processor, combine the cooked edamame, tahini, minced garlic, lemon juice, olive oil, ground cumin, smoked paprika, salt, and pepper.

Blend Until Smooth: Pulse the mixture until smooth, scraping down the sides of the food processor as needed.

If the mixture is too thick, add water, 1 tablespoon at a time, until you reach your desired consistency.

Adjust Seasoning: Taste the hummus and adjust the seasoning with more salt, pepper, or lemon juice if needed. Blend again to incorporate.

Serve: Transfer the edamame hummus to a serving bowl. Drizzle with a little extra olive oil and sprinkle with additional smoked paprika for garnish if desired.

Serving Suggestions:

Serve with raw vegetable sticks like carrots, celery, cucumber, and bell peppers for a nutritious snack or appetizer. Spread on whole grain crackers or toast as a healthy sandwich or wrap filling.

Nutritional Information (per serving - 2 tablespoons):

Calories: 70 kcal
Total Fat: 4.5 grams
Saturated Fat: 0.5 grams
Sodium: 55 mg

Total Carbohydrates: 4 grams
Dietary Fiber: 2 grams
Sugars: 0.5 grams
Protein: 4 grams

Appetizers for Entertaining

Caprese Salad Skewers

Yield: 4 servings
Preparation Time: 15 minutes
Cooking Time: 0 minutes

Ingredients:

- 200 grams cherry tomatoes
- 200 grams fresh mozzarella cheese, cut into bite-sized cubes
- 1 bunch fresh basil leaves
- 2 tablespoons extra virgin olive oil
- 1 tablespoon balsamic vinegar
- Salt and pepper to taste
- 8 wooden skewers

Instructions:

Prepare Ingredients: Rinse the cherry tomatoes and basil leaves. Drain any excess water. Cut the fresh mozzarella cheese into bite-sized cubes.
Assemble Skewers: Thread the cherry tomatoes, mozzarella cheese cubes, and basil leaves onto the wooden skewers, alternating between ingredients.

Season: Arrange the assembled skewers on a serving platter. Drizzle with extra virgin olive oil and balsamic vinegar. Season with salt and pepper to taste.
Serve: Serve immediately as a heart-healthy appetizer or side dish.

Tips:
Use ripe cherry tomatoes and fresh mozzarella cheese for the best flavor.

Soak the wooden skewers in water for 15-20 minutes before assembling to prevent them from burning during grilling.

Nutritional Information (per serving - 2 skewers):

Calories: 190 kcal
Total Fat: 15 grams
Saturated Fat: 6 grams
Cholesterol: 30 mg
Sodium: 220 mg

Total Carbohydrates: 5 grams
Dietary Fiber: 1 gram
Sugars: 3 grams
Protein: 10 grams

Fresh Fruit Kabobs with Yogurt Dip

Yield: 4 servings
Preparation Time: 15 minutes
Cooking Time: 0 minutes

Ingredients:

- 200 grams strawberries, hulled and halved
- 200 grams pineapple, cut into chunks
- 200 grams grapes (red or green)
- 2 ripe bananas, peeled and sliced

- 200 grams low-fat Greek yogurt
- 1 tablespoon honey
- 1 teaspoon vanilla extract
- Wooden skewers

Instructions:
Prepare Ingredients: Wash all fruits thoroughly. Hull and halve the strawberries. Cut the pineapple into chunks. Rinse the grapes and remove any stems. Peel and slice the bananas.
Assemble Kabobs: Thread the fruit onto the wooden skewers in any order you prefer, alternating between different fruits.

Prepare Yogurt Dip: In a small bowl, mix the Greek yogurt, honey, and vanilla extract until well combined. Adjust sweetness to taste by adding more honey if desired.
Serve: Arrange the fruit kabobs on a serving platter alongside the yogurt dip.

Tips:
Use a variety of colorful fruits for visual appeal and a diverse range of nutrients.

If using wooden skewers, soak them in water for 15-20 minutes before assembling to prevent them from splintering.

Nutritional Information (per serving):

Calories: 150 kcal
Total Fat: 1 gram
Saturated Fat: 0 grams
Cholesterol: 0 mg
Sodium: 20 mg

Total Carbohydrates: 32 grams
Dietary Fiber: 4 grams
Sugars: 23 grams
Protein: 5 grams

Greek Yogurt and Berry Popsicles

Yield: 6 servings

Preparation Time: 10 minutes
Freezing Time: 4 hours

Ingredients:

- 300 grams plain low-fat Greek yogurt
- 150 grams mixed berries (strawberries, blueberries, raspberries)
- 2 tablespoons honey (optional)
- 1 teaspoon vanilla extract

Instructions:
Prepare Berries: Wash the berries thoroughly and pat them dry with a paper towel. If using strawberries, hull and chop them into small pieces.
Mix Yogurt Mixture: In a mixing bowl, combine the Greek yogurt, honey (if using), and vanilla extract. Stir until smooth and well combined.
Layer Yogurt and Berries: Spoon a small amount of the yogurt mixture into each popsicle mold, filling them about one-third full. Add a layer of mixed berries on top of the yogurt. Repeat the layers until the molds are almost full, leaving a little space at the top.

Insert Sticks: Place the popsicle sticks into the molds, ensuring they are centered in the mixture. Tap the molds gently on the counter to remove any air bubbles.
Freeze: Transfer the popsicle molds to the freezer and let them freeze for at least 4 hours or until completely solid.
Serve: Once frozen, remove the popsicles from the molds by running them under warm water for a few seconds. Serve immediately and enjoy!

Tips:
Feel free to use any combination of berries according to your preference and availability.

For added sweetness, you can adjust the amount of honey to suit your taste.
If you don't have popsicle molds, you can use small paper cups and wooden popsicle sticks as an alternative.

Nutritional Information (per serving):

Calories: 70 kcal
Total Fat: 0.5 grams
Saturated Fat: 0 grams
Cholesterol: 2 mg
Sodium: 15 mg

Total Carbohydrates: 10 grams
Dietary Fiber: 1.5 grams
Sugars: 8 grams
Protein: 6 grams

Cherry Tomato and Mozzarella Bites

Yield: 4 servings
Preparation Time: 15 minutes

Ingredients:

- 200 grams cherry tomatoes
- 200 grams fresh mozzarella cheese, cut into small cubes
- 2 tablespoons extra-virgin olive oil
- 2 tablespoons balsamic glaze
- Fresh basil leaves, for garnish
- Salt and black pepper to taste

Instructions:
Prepare Ingredients: Wash the cherry tomatoes and pat them dry with a paper towel. Cut each cherry tomato in half. Cut the fresh mozzarella cheese into small cubes.

Assemble Bites: Take a toothpick and skewer a cherry tomato half followed by a cube of mozzarella cheese. Repeat until all cherry tomatoes and mozzarella cheese cubes are used.

Drizzle with Olive Oil: Arrange the tomato and mozzarella skewers on a serving platter. Drizzle them with extra-virgin olive oil.
Season: Season the bites with a pinch of salt and black pepper to taste.

Garnish: Drizzle the balsamic glaze over the tomato and mozzarella bites. Garnish with fresh basil leaves.
Serve: Arrange the cherry tomato and mozzarella bites on a serving platter and serve immediately.

Tips:

Choose ripe cherry tomatoes and fresh mozzarella cheese for the best flavor.
You can use toothpicks or small skewers to assemble the bites.

For added flavor, sprinkle some dried Italian herbs or chili flakes before serving.

Nutritional Information (per serving):

Calories: 180 kcal
Total Fat: 14 grams
Saturated Fat: 6 grams
Cholesterol: 30 mg
Sodium: 200 mg

Total Carbohydrates: 5 grams
Dietary Fiber: 1 gram
Sugars: 3 grams
Protein: 10 grams

Avocado Deviled Eggs

Yield: 4 servings
Preparation Time: 15 minutes
Cooking Time: 10 minutes

Ingredients:

- 4 large eggs
- 1 ripe avocado
- 1 tablespoon Greek yogurt
- 1 teaspoon Dijon mustard
- 1 teaspoon lemon juice
- Salt and black pepper to taste
- Paprika and chopped chives, for garnish

Instructions:

Boil the Eggs: Place the eggs in a saucepan and cover them with cold water. Bring the water to a boil over medium-high heat. Once boiling, cover the saucepan and remove it from the heat. Let the eggs sit in the hot water for 10 minutes. Then, transfer them to a bowl of ice water to cool.
Peel and Halve the Eggs: Once the eggs are cool, peel them and cut them in half lengthwise. Carefully remove the yolks and place them in a mixing bowl. Set the egg white halves aside.
Prepare the Filling: Cut the avocado in half and remove the pit. Scoop the avocado flesh into the mixing bowl

with the egg yolks. Add Greek yogurt, Dijon mustard, and lemon juice to the bowl. Mash everything together until smooth and creamy. Season with salt and black pepper to taste.
Fill the Egg Whites: Spoon the avocado mixture into the hollows of the egg white halves, dividing it evenly among them.
Garnish and Serve: Sprinkle the filled egg halves with paprika and chopped chives for garnish.
Serve: Arrange the avocado deviled eggs on a serving platter and serve immediately, or refrigerate until ready to serve.

Tips:

Use ripe avocados for the creamiest texture.
Adjust the seasoning to your taste preferences by adding more lemon juice, mustard, or salt if needed.

For a smoother filling, you can use a food processor instead of mashing the ingredients by hand.

Nutritional Information (per serving):

Calories: 110 kcal
Total Fat: 8 grams
Saturated Fat: 2 grams
Cholesterol: 95 mg
Sodium: 90 mg

Total Carbohydrates: 4 grams
Dietary Fiber: 3 grams
Sugars: 0.5 grams
Protein: 6 grams

Spicy Edamame Beans

Yield: 4 servings
Preparation Time: 10 minutes
Cooking Time: 10 minutes

Ingredients:

- 400 grams edamame beans (shelled)
- 1 tablespoon olive oil
- 2 cloves garlic, minced
- 1 teaspoon chili powder
- 1/2 teaspoon paprika
- 1/4 teaspoon cayenne pepper (adjust to taste)
- Salt to taste
- Freshly ground black pepper to taste
- 1 tablespoon lime juice
- 1 tablespoon chopped fresh cilantro (optional, for garnish)

Instructions:

Prepare the Edamame Beans: If using frozen edamame beans, thaw them according to package instructions. If using fresh edamame, shell them and set aside.

Steam the Edamame Beans: Bring a pot of water to a boil. Add the edamame beans and cook for 3-5 minutes until tender. Drain and set aside.

Season the Beans: In a large skillet, heat olive oil over medium heat. Add minced garlic and sauté for 1-2 minutes until fragrant.

Add Spices: Add chili powder, paprika, cayenne pepper, salt, and black pepper to the skillet. Stir well to combine with the garlic.

Cook the Edamame: Add the steamed edamame beans to the skillet. Toss to coat them evenly with the spicy

mixture. Cook for an additional 2-3 minutes, stirring occasionally, until the beans are heated through and well-coated with the spices.

Finish and Serve: Remove the skillet from the heat. Drizzle lime juice over the spicy edamame beans and toss gently. Garnish with chopped fresh cilantro if desired.

Serve: Transfer the spicy edamame beans to a serving dish and serve hot as a nutritious appetizer or snack.

Tips:

Adjust the level of spiciness by increasing or decreasing the amount of cayenne pepper.

You can customize the seasoning by adding other spices like garlic powder, onion powder, or cumin.

For added flavour, sprinkle nutritional yeast or grated Parmesan cheese over the cooked beans before serving.

Nutritional Information (per serving):

Calories: 140 kcal
Total Fat: 7 grams
Saturated Fat: 1 gram
Cholesterol: 0 mg
Sodium: 200 mg

Total Carbohydrates: 10 grams
Dietary Fiber: 6 grams
Sugars: 2 grams
Protein: 10 grams

Easy finger foods

Baked Sweet Potato Fries

Yield: 4 servings
Preparation Time: 15 minutes

Cooking Time: 25 minutes

Ingredients:

- 600 grams sweet potatoes (about 2 large sweet potatoes), peeled and cut into fries
- 2 tablespoons olive oil
- 1 teaspoon garlic powder
- 1 teaspoon paprika
- 1/2 teaspoon onion powder
- 1/2 teaspoon ground cumin
- Salt to taste
- Freshly ground black pepper to taste
- Chopped fresh parsley or cilantro for garnish (optional)

Instructions:

Preheat the Oven: Preheat your oven to 220°C (425°F). Line a large baking sheet with parchment paper or lightly grease it with olive oil.

Prepare the Sweet Potatoes: Wash, peel, and cut the sweet potatoes into evenly sized fries, about 1/2-inch thick.

Season the Fries: In a large bowl, toss the sweet potato fries with olive oil, garlic powder, paprika, onion powder, ground cumin, salt, and black pepper until evenly coated.

Arrange on Baking Sheet: Spread the seasoned sweet potato fries in a single layer on the prepared baking sheet, making sure they are not overcrowded. This ensures they crisp up evenly.

Bake the Fries: Place the baking sheet in the preheated oven and bake for 20-25 minutes, flipping the fries halfway through, until they are golden brown and crispy on the outside.

Garnish and Serve: Once the sweet potato fries are done, remove them from the oven and let them cool slightly. Garnish with chopped fresh parsley or cilantro if desired, and serve warm.

Tips:

For extra crispiness, you can soak the sweet potato fries in cold water for about 30 minutes before baking. Pat them dry thoroughly before seasoning and baking.

Feel free to adjust the seasoning according to your taste preferences. You can add a pinch of cayenne pepper for a spicy kick or a sprinkle of smoked paprika for a smoky flavor.

Serve the sweet potato fries with a side of low-fat Greek yogurt mixed with lime juice and chopped herbs for a delicious dipping sauce.

Nutritional Information (per serving):

Calories: 180 kcal
Total Fat: 7 grams
Saturated Fat: 1 gram
Cholesterol: 0 mg
Sodium: 200 mg

Total Carbohydrates: 28 grams
Dietary Fiber: 4 grams
Sugars: 6 grams
Protein: 2 grams

Mini Quinoa and Spinach Patties

Yield: 12 patties
Preparation Time: 15 minutes
Cooking Time: 20 minutes

Ingredients:

- 1 cup cooked quinoa
- 150 grams fresh spinach, chopped
- 1 small onion, finely diced
- 2 cloves garlic, minced
- 2 tablespoons whole wheat flour
- 1 tablespoon nutritional yeast (optional)
- 1 tablespoon ground flaxseed
- 2 tablespoons water
- 1 teaspoon dried oregano
- 1/2 teaspoon paprika
- Salt to taste
- Black pepper to taste
- Olive oil for cooking

Instructions:

Prepare Quinoa: Cook quinoa according to package instructions and let it cool to room temperature.

Cook Spinach: In a skillet, heat a teaspoon of olive oil over medium heat. Add chopped spinach and cook until wilted, about 2-3 minutes. Remove from heat and let it cool.

Mix Flaxseed: In a small bowl, mix ground flaxseed with water and set aside to thicken for 5 minutes.

Combine Ingredients: In a large mixing bowl, combine cooked quinoa, cooked spinach, diced onion, minced garlic, whole wheat flour, nutritional yeast (if using), oregano, paprika, salt, and black pepper. Add the flaxseed mixture and mix until well combined.

Form Patties: Divide the mixture into 12 equal portions and shape each portion into a small patty, about 2 inches in diameter and 1/2 inch thick.

Cook Patties: Heat a non-stick skillet over medium heat and add a tablespoon of olive oil. Place the patties in the skillet and cook for 4-5 minutes on each side, until golden brown and crispy.

Serve: Once cooked, transfer the patties to a serving plate. Serve warm as a nutritious appetizer or snack.

Nutritional Information (per serving - 1 patty):

Calories: 70 kcal
Total Fat: 2 grams
Saturated Fat: 0 grams
Cholesterol: 0 mg Sodium: 60 mg

Total Carbohydrates: 10 grams
Dietary Fiber: 2 grams
Sugars: 1 gram
Protein: 3 grams

Carrot and Zucchini Muffins

Yield: 12 muffins
Preparation Time: 15 minutes
Cooking Time: 25 minutes

Ingredients:

- 200 grams whole wheat flour
- 100 grams rolled oats
- 2 teaspoons baking powder
- 1/2 teaspoon baking soda
- 1/2 teaspoon ground cinnamon
- 1/4 teaspoon ground nutmeg
- 1/4 teaspoon salt
- 2 large eggs
- 120 milliliters unsweetened applesauce
- 80 milliliters olive oil
- 80 milliliters honey or maple syrup
- 1 teaspoon vanilla extract
- 150 grams grated carrot (about 1 large carrot)
- 150 grams grated zucchini (about 1 small zucchini)
- 50 grams chopped walnuts (optional)

Instructions:

Preheat Oven: Preheat your oven to 180°C (350°F). Line a muffin tin with paper liners or lightly grease the cups with oil.

Mix Dry Ingredients: In a large mixing bowl, combine the whole wheat flour, rolled oats, baking powder, baking soda, cinnamon, nutmeg, and salt. Stir until well combined.

Prepare Wet Ingredients: In another bowl, whisk together the eggs, applesauce, olive oil, honey or maple syrup, and vanilla extract until smooth.

Combine Ingredients: Pour the wet ingredients into the dry ingredients and stir until just combined. Be careful not to overmix. Fold in the grated carrot, grated zucchini, and chopped walnuts (if using) until evenly distributed.

Fill Muffin Cups: Divide the batter evenly among the muffin cups, filling each cup about 2/3 full.

Bake: Place the muffin tin in the preheated oven and bake for 20-25 minutes, or until a toothpick inserted into the center of a muffin comes out clean.

Cool and Serve: Remove the muffins from the oven and allow them to cool in the tin for 5 minutes before transferring them to a wire rack to cool completely. Serve warm or at room temperature.

Nutritional Information (per serving - 1 muffin):

Calories: 180 kcal
Total Fat: 7 grams
Saturated Fat: 1 gram
Cholesterol: 31 mg

Sodium: 180 mg
Total Carbohydrates: 26 grams
Dietary Fiber: 3 grams
Sugars: 9 grams

Protein: 4 grams

Kale Chips with Sea Salt

Yield: 4 servings
Preparation Time: 10 minutes
Cooking Time: 15 minutes

Ingredients:

- 200 grams kale leaves, stems removed and torn into bite-sized pieces
- 15 milliliters olive oil
- Sea salt, to taste

Instructions:
Preheat Oven: Preheat your oven to 150°C (300°F) and line a baking sheet with parchment paper.
Prepare Kale: Wash the kale leaves thoroughly and pat them dry with a clean kitchen towel or paper towels. Make sure the leaves are completely dry to ensure crispy chips.
Massage with Oil: In a large bowl, drizzle the kale leaves with olive oil. Use your hands to massage the oil into the leaves, ensuring they are evenly coated.
Season with Salt: Sprinkle the kale leaves with sea salt, adjusting the amount to your taste preferences. Toss the leaves to ensure the salt is evenly distributed.

Arrange on Baking Sheet: Arrange the kale leaves in a single layer on the prepared baking sheet, making sure they are not overlapping.
Bake: Place the baking sheet in the preheated oven and bake for 10-15 minutes, or until the kale leaves are crispy but not burnt. Keep an eye on them as they can burn quickly.
Cool and Serve: Remove the kale chips from the oven and let them cool on the baking sheet for a few minutes before transferring them to a serving bowl. Serve immediately as a healthy snack.

Nutritional Information (per serving):

Calories: 50 kcal
Total Fat: 3 grams
Saturated Fat: 0.5 grams
Cholesterol: 0 mg
Sodium: 150 mg

Total Carbohydrates: 5 grams
Dietary Fiber: 1.5 grams
Sugars: 0 grams
Protein: 2 grams

Cucumber and Avocado Sushi Rolls

Yield: 4 servings
Preparation Time: 20 minutes
Cooking Time: 0 minutes

Ingredients:

- 200 grams sushi rice
- 4 sheets nori (seaweed)
- 1 ripe avocado, thinly sliced
- 1 cucumber, julienned
- 30 milliliters rice vinegar

- 5 milliliters mirin (optional)
- 5 milliliters soy sauce (low-sodium)
- 5 milliliters sesame oil
- Sesame seeds, for garnish

Instructions:

Prepare Sushi Rice: Rinse the sushi rice in cold water until the water runs clear. Cook the rice according to package instructions. Once cooked, transfer the rice to a large bowl and add rice vinegar (mixed with mirin, if using) while the rice is still hot. Gently mix to combine and let it cool to room temperature.

Prepare Cucumber and Avocado: Julienne the cucumber into thin strips. Peel the avocado, remove the pit, and thinly slice it.

Assemble Sushi Rolls: Place a sheet of nori on a bamboo sushi mat or a clean kitchen towel. With wet hands, spread an even layer of sushi rice onto the nori, leaving a small border at the top edge. Arrange cucumber and avocado slices evenly across the rice.

Roll Sushi: Starting from the bottom edge, tightly roll the nori sheet around the fillings, using the sushi mat or towel to help shape it into a cylinder. Seal the edge by moistening it with water.

Slice Rolls: Use a sharp knife to slice the sushi roll into bite-sized pieces, wiping the knife clean with a damp cloth between cuts to keep the edges clean.

Serve: Arrange the sushi rolls on a serving platter, sprinkle with sesame seeds, and drizzle with a mixture of soy sauce and sesame oil for added flavor.

Nutritional Information (per serving):

Calories: 220 kcal
Total Fat: 8 grams
Saturated Fat: 1 gram
Cholesterol: 0 mg
Sodium: 100 mg

Total Carbohydrates: 32 grams
Dietary Fiber: 5 grams
Sugars: 1 gram
Protein: 4 grams

Broccoli and Cheddar Bites

Yield: 12 servings
Preparation Time: 15 minutes
Cooking Time: 20 minutes

Ingredients:

- 300 grams broccoli florets
- 100 grams cheddar cheese, grated
- 2 eggs
- 30 milliliters low-fat milk
- 30 grams whole wheat breadcrumbs
- 5 grams garlic powder
- Salt and pepper, to taste
- Cooking spray

Instructions:

Preheat Oven: Preheat your oven to 180°C (350°F). Lightly grease a mini muffin tin with cooking spray and set aside.

Steam Broccoli: Steam the broccoli florets until tender, about 5-7 minutes. Once cooked, drain any excess water and roughly chop the broccoli into smaller pieces.

Prepare Batter: In a large mixing bowl, whisk together the eggs and milk. Add the chopped broccoli, grated cheddar cheese, whole wheat breadcrumbs, garlic powder, salt, and pepper. Mix until well combined.

Fill Muffin Tin: Spoon the broccoli mixture evenly into the prepared mini muffin tin, filling each cavity to the top.

Bake: Transfer the muffin tin to the preheated oven and bake for 15-20 minutes, or until the broccoli and cheddar bites are set and lightly golden on top.

Cool and Serve: Allow the bites to cool in the muffin tin for a few minutes before carefully removing them. Serve warm or at room temperature.

Nutritional Information (per serving):

Calories: 70 kcal
Total Fat: 4 grams
Saturated Fat: 2 grams
Cholesterol: 40 mg
Sodium: 100 mg

Total Carbohydrates: 4 grams
Dietary Fiber: 1 gram
Sugars: 1 gram
Protein: 5 grams

Apple Slices with Almond Butter

Yield: 2 servings
Preparation Time: 5 minutes
Cooking Time: 0 minutes

Ingredients:

- 2 medium apples (preferably Granny Smith or Honeycrisp)
- 4 tablespoons almond butter
- 1 tablespoon honey (optional)
- Cinnamon powder, for garnish (optional)

Instructions:

Prepare Apples: Wash the apples thoroughly under running water and pat them dry with a kitchen towel. Core the apples and cut them into slices.

Serve with Almond Butter: Arrange the apple slices on a serving plate. Place the almond butter in a small bowl and serve it alongside the apple slices.

Optional Sweetener: Drizzle honey over the almond butter if desired, for added sweetness.

Garnish: Sprinkle a pinch of cinnamon powder over the almond butter for extra flavor and aroma.

Nutritional Information (per serving

Calories: 220 kcal
Total Fat: 15 grams
Saturated Fat: 1.5 grams
Cholesterol: 0 mg
Sodium: 5 mg

Total Carbohydrates: 20 grams
Dietary Fiber: 6 grams
Sugars: 14 grams
Protein: 5 grams

Desserts and Treats

Low-Fat and Low-Sugar Desserts

Dark Chocolate Covered Strawberries

Yield: 12 servings
Preparation time: 10 minutes
Cooking time: 5 minutes
Total time: 15 minutes

Ingredients:

- 200g dark chocolate (70% cocoa or higher), chopped
- 250g fresh strawberries, washed and dried

Instructions:

Prepare the Strawberries:
Wash the strawberries thoroughly under cold water.
Pat them dry with a clean kitchen towel or paper towels.
Make sure they are completely dry as any moisture can affect the chocolate coating.
Melt the Dark Chocolate:
Fill a small saucepan with water and bring it to a simmer over medium heat.
Place a heatproof bowl over the saucepan, ensuring that the bottom of the bowl doesn't touch the water.
Add the chopped dark chocolate to the bowl and gently stir until melted and smooth.
Coat the Strawberries:
Hold each strawberry by the stem and dip it into the melted chocolate, swirling to coat about three-quarters of the berry.

Lift the strawberry out of the chocolate and allow any excess to drip off.
Set the Chocolate:
Place the chocolate-coated strawberries onto a parchment-lined baking sheet or plate.
Chill:
Place the baking sheet in the refrigerator for about 10-15 minutes to allow the chocolate to set.
Serve:
Once the chocolate is set, transfer the strawberries to a serving platter.
Serve immediately or store in the refrigerator until ready to serve.

Nutritional Information (Per Serving):

Calories: 80 kcal
Total Fat: 5g
Saturated Fat: 3g
Cholesterol: 0mg Sodium: 0mg

Total Carbohydrates: 8g
Dietary Fiber: 2g
Total Sugars: 5g
Protein: 1g

Chia Seed Pudding with Mango

Yield: 4 servings
Preparation time: 10 minutes
Chilling time: 4 hours or overnight
Total time: 4 hours 10 minutes (including chilling time)

Ingredients:

- 60g chia seeds
- 480ml unsweetened almond milk
- 1 tablespoon maple syrup (optional)
- 1 teaspoon vanilla extract
- 1 ripe mango, peeled and diced
- Fresh mint leaves for garnish (optional)

Instructions:
Prepare the Chia Seed Mixture:
In a mixing bowl, combine the chia seeds, unsweetened almond milk, maple syrup (if using), and vanilla extract. Whisk the ingredients together until well combined. Let the mixture sit for about 5 minutes, then whisk again to prevent clumping.
Chill the Mixture:
Cover the bowl with plastic wrap or transfer the mixture to individual serving jars.
Place in the refrigerator to chill for at least 4 hours or overnight. The chia seeds will absorb the liquid and thicken to a pudding-like consistency.

Prepare the Mango:
Just before serving, peel and dice the ripe mango.
Assemble the Pudding:
Divide the chilled chia seed pudding into serving bowls or glasses.
Top each serving with a portion of diced mango.
Garnish and Serve:
Garnish with fresh mint leaves if desired.
Serve chilled and enjoy!

Nutritional Information (Per Serving):

Calories: 140 kcal
Total Fat: 6g
Saturated Fat: 0.5g
Cholesterol: 0mg
Sodium: 80mg

Total Carbohydrates: 19g
Dietary Fiber: 10g
Total Sugars: 7g
Protein: 4g

Baked Apples with Cinnamon

Yield: 4 servings
Preparation time: 10 minutes
Cooking time: 30 minutes
Total time: 40 minutes

Ingredients:

- 4 medium-sized apples (about 600g)
- 2 tablespoons (30g) unsalted butter or coconut oil, melted
- 2 tablespoons (30ml) maple syrup or honey
- 1 teaspoon ground cinnamon
- 30g chopped walnuts or almonds (optional)
- Greek yogurt or low-fat vanilla ice cream for serving (optional)

Instructions:
Preheat the Oven:
Preheat your oven to 180°C (350°F). Line a baking dish with parchment paper or lightly grease it with cooking spray.
Prepare the Apples:
Wash the apples thoroughly and pat them dry with a kitchen towel.
Core each apple using an apple corer or a small knife, leaving the bottom intact to create a well for the filling.
Mix the Filling:

In a small bowl, mix together the melted butter or coconut oil, maple syrup or honey, and ground cinnamon until well combined.
Fill the Apples:
Place the cored apples in the prepared baking dish.
Spoon the cinnamon mixture evenly into the wells of the apples.
If using, sprinkle the chopped walnuts or almonds over the top of each apple.
Bake the Apples:

Transfer the baking dish to the preheated oven. Bake for about 25-30 minutes or until the apples are tender and lightly golden brown.

Serve Warm:

Remove the baked apples from the oven and let them cool slightly.
Serve warm as is or with a dollop of Greek yogurt or a scoop of low-fat vanilla ice cream if desired.

Nutritional Information (Per Serving, without optional toppings):

Calories: 160 kcal
Total Fat: 6g
Saturated Fat: 3g
Cholesterol: 10mg
Sodium: 0mg

Total Carbohydrates: 28g
Dietary Fiber: 5g
Total Sugars: 20g
Protein: 1g

Avocado Chocolate Mousse

Yield: 4 servings
Preparation time: 10 minutes
Chilling time: 1 hour
Total time: 1 hour 10 minutes

Ingredients:

- 2 ripe avocados, peeled and pitted (about 300g each)
- 75g unsweetened cocoa powder
- 120ml unsweetened almond milk or any milk of choice
- 60ml pure maple syrup or honey
- 1 teaspoon pure vanilla extract
- Fresh berries, for serving (optional)
- Mint leaves, for garnish (optional)

Instructions:

Prepare the Avocado:
Cut the ripe avocados in half, remove the pits, and scoop out the flesh into a blender or food processor.

: Blend the Ingredients
Add the unsweetened cocoa powder, almond milk, maple syrup or honey, and vanilla extract to the blender or food processor with the avocado.
Blend Until Smooth:
Blend the mixture on high speed until smooth and creamy, scraping down the sides of the blender or food processor as needed to ensure everything is well combined.

Chill the Mousse:
Transfer the avocado chocolate mousse to a bowl or individual serving glasses.
Cover the bowl or glasses with plastic wrap and refrigerate for at least 1 hour to chill and firm up the mousse.

Serve and Garnish:
Once chilled, remove the mousse from the refrigerator.
Serve the avocado chocolate mousse chilled, topped with fresh berries and mint leaves if desired.

Nutritional Information (Per Serving, without optional toppings):

Calories: 210 kcal
Total Fat: 14g
Saturated Fat: 2g
Cholesterol: 0mg
Sodium: 10mg

Total Carbohydrates: 24g
Dietary Fiber: 8g
Total Sugars: 12g
Protein: 4g

Lemon and Blueberry Sorbet

Yield: 6 servings
Preparation time: 10 minutes
Freezing time: 4 hours
Total time: 4 hours 10 minutes

Ingredients:

- 500g fresh or frozen blueberries
- 120ml freshly squeezed lemon juice (about 3-4 lemons)
- Zest of 1 lemon
- 120ml water
- 60g honey or maple syrup (adjust to taste)
- Fresh mint leaves, for garnish (optional)

Instructions:
Prepare the Blueberries:
If using fresh blueberries, rinse them under cold water and pat dry with a paper towel. If using frozen blueberries, thaw them at room temperature for about 10-15 minutes.
Blend the Ingredients:
In a blender or food processor, combine the blueberries, freshly squeezed lemon juice, lemon zest, water, and honey or maple syrup.
Blend Until Smooth:
Blend the mixture on high speed until smooth and well combined, scraping down the sides of the blender or food processor as needed.
Strain (Optional):
For a smoother texture, you can strain the mixture through a fine-mesh sieve to remove any blueberry skins or pulp. This step is optional.

Transfer to Freezer-Safe Container:
Pour the blended blueberry mixture into a freezer-safe container or shallow dish.
Freeze the Sorbet:
Cover the container with a lid or plastic wrap and place it in the freezer.
Allow the sorbet to freeze for at least 4 hours or until firm, stirring or fluffing with a fork every hour to prevent ice crystals from forming.
Serve and Garnish:
Once the sorbet is fully frozen, remove it from the freezer and let it sit at room temperature for a few minutes to soften slightly.
Scoop the lemon and blueberry sorbet into serving bowls or glasses.
Garnish with fresh mint leaves if desired.

Nutritional Information (Per Serving):

Calories: 90 kcal
Total Fat: 0.3g
Saturated Fat: 0g
Cholesterol: 0mg
Sodium: 1mg

Total Carbohydrates: 23g
Dietary Fiber: 3g
Total Sugars: 18g
Protein: 1g

Fresh Fruit Salad with Mint

Yield: 4 servings
Preparation time: 15 minutes
Total time: 15 minutes

Ingredients:

- 200g strawberries, hulled and sliced
- 200g blueberries
- 200g raspberries
- 1 large mango, peeled and diced

- 1 medium orange, peeled and segmented
- 1 tablespoon honey or maple syrup (optional)
- Juice of 1 lime
- 2 tablespoons fresh mint leaves, chopped

Instructions:

Prepare the Fruit:
Wash all the fruits thoroughly under cold running water. Hull and slice the strawberries, and peel and dice the mango. Peel the orange and separate it into segments.

Combine the Fruits:
In a large mixing bowl, combine the sliced strawberries, blueberries, raspberries, diced mango, and orange segments.

Add Sweetener and Lime Juice:
If desired, drizzle the honey or maple syrup over the fruit for a touch of sweetness. Squeeze the juice of one lime over the fruit mixture.

Toss Gently:

Using a spatula or spoon, gently toss the fruit together until evenly combined and coated with the lime juice. Be careful not to crush the delicate berries.

Add Mint Leaves:
Sprinkle the chopped fresh mint leaves over the fruit salad.

Chill and Serve:
Cover the bowl with plastic wrap or transfer the fruit salad to a serving dish. Chill in the refrigerator for at least 30 minutes to allow the flavors to meld together.

Serve Cold:
Serve the heart-healthy fresh fruit salad cold, garnished with additional mint leaves if desired.

Nutritional Information (Per Serving):

Calories: 120 kcal
Total Fat: 0.6g
Saturated Fat: 0.1g
Cholesterol: 0mg
Sodium: 2mg

Total Carbohydrates: 30g
Dietary Fiber: 7g
Total Sugars: 21g
Protein: 2g

Raspberry Chia Jam Bars

Yield: 12 bars
Preparation time: 15 minutes
Cooking time: 25 minutes
Chilling time: 2 hours

Ingredients:

- **For the Raspberry Chia Jam:**
- 300g fresh raspberries
- 3 tablespoons chia seeds
- 2 tablespoons maple syrup or honey
- 1 teaspoon vanilla extract
- **For the Oatmeal Crust and Topping:**

- 150g rolled oats
- 75g whole wheat flour
- 60g unsalted butter, melted
- 3 tablespoons maple syrup or honey
- 1 teaspoon vanilla extract
- 1/4 teaspoon salt

Instructions:
Preheat the Oven:
Preheat your oven to 180°C (350°F). Grease or line an 8x8-inch baking dish with parchment paper, leaving some overhang for easy removal.

Prepare the Raspberry Chia Jam:
In a saucepan, combine the fresh raspberries, chia seeds, maple syrup (or honey), and vanilla extract. Cook over medium heat, stirring occasionally, until the raspberries break down and the mixture thickens, about 10-12 minutes. Remove from heat and let it cool slightly.

Make the Oatmeal Crust and Topping:
In a large mixing bowl, combine the rolled oats, whole wheat flour, melted butter, maple syrup (or honey), vanilla extract, and salt. Mix until well combined and the mixture resembles coarse crumbs.

Assemble the Bars:

Press two-thirds of the oatmeal mixture firmly into the bottom of the prepared baking dish to form the crust. Spread the raspberry chia jam evenly over the oatmeal crust.

Add the Topping:
Sprinkle the remaining oatmeal mixture evenly over the raspberry chia jam layer, forming the topping.

Bake:
Place the baking dish in the preheated oven and bake for 25-30 minutes, or until the topping is golden brown.

Cool and Chill:
Remove the baking dish from the oven and let the raspberry chia jam bars cool completely in the dish. Once cooled, transfer to the refrigerator and chill for at least 2 hours to firm up.

Slice and Serve:

Use the parchment paper overhang to lift the chilled bars out of the baking dish. Slice into 12 bars and serve chilled or at room temperature.

Nutritional Information (Per Serving):

Calories: 150 kcal
Total Fat: 5g
Saturated Fat: 2g
Cholesterol: 8mg
Sodium: 51mg

Total Carbohydrates: 24g
Dietary Fiber: 4g
Total Sugars: 9g
Protein: 3g

Pineapple Coconut Smoothie

Yield: 2 servings
Preparation time: 5 minutes
Cooking time: 0 minutes

Ingredients:

- 200g fresh pineapple, peeled and chopped
- 120ml unsweetened coconut milk
- 120ml plain Greek yogurt
- 30g shredded unsweetened coconut
- 1 tablespoon honey (optional)
- Juice of 1/2 lime
- 1/2 teaspoon vanilla extract
- 4-6 ice cubes

Instructions:
Prepare the Ingredients:
Peel and chop the fresh pineapple into chunks. Measure out the coconut milk, Greek yogurt, shredded coconut, honey (if using), lime juice, and vanilla extract.
Blend the Ingredients:
In a blender, combine the chopped pineapple, coconut milk, Greek yogurt, shredded coconut, honey (if using), lime juice, vanilla extract, and ice cubes.
Blend Until Smooth:
Blend the ingredients on high speed until smooth and creamy, scraping down the sides of the blender as needed to ensure all ingredients are well incorporated.

Adjust Consistency (Optional):
If the smoothie is too thick, add a splash more coconut milk or water and blend again until desired consistency is reached.
Serve:
Pour the pineapple coconut smoothie into glasses and garnish with additional shredded coconut or a wedge of pineapple, if desired.
Enjoy:
Serve immediately and enjoy this refreshing and heart-healthy smoothie as a nutritious snack or breakfast option.

Nutritional Information (Per Serving):

Calories: 180 kcal
Total Fat: 9g
Saturated Fat: 7g
Cholesterol: 2mg

Sodium: 33mg
Total Carbohydrates: 21g
Dietary Fiber: 2g
Total Sugars: 16g
Protein: 6g

Apple Cinnamon Rice Pudding

Yield: 4 servings
Preparation time: 10 minutes
Cooking time: 30 minutes

Ingredients:

- 1 cup (185g) short-grain brown rice
- 2 cups (480ml) unsweetened almond milk
- 1 cup (240ml) water
- 2 medium apples, peeled, cored, and diced
- 2 tablespoons (30ml) maple syrup
- 1 teaspoon ground cinnamon
- 1/4 teaspoon ground nutmeg
- 1/4 teaspoon salt
- 1 teaspoon vanilla extract
- 2 tablespoons (30g) chopped walnuts (optional, for garnish)

Instructions:

Prepare the Rice:
Rinse the brown rice under cold water until the water runs clear. Drain well.

Cook the Rice:
In a medium saucepan, combine the rinsed rice, almond milk, and water. Bring to a boil over medium-high heat. Reduce the heat to low, cover, and simmer for 25-30 minutes, or until the rice is tender and most of the liquid is absorbed.

Add Apples and Sweeteners:
Stir in the diced apples, maple syrup, ground cinnamon, ground nutmeg, and salt. Continue to cook, uncovered, for an additional 5-7 minutes, or until the apples are tender and the mixture has thickened to your desired consistency.

Finish with Vanilla:
Remove the rice pudding from the heat and stir in the vanilla extract.

Serve:
Divide the apple cinnamon rice pudding among serving bowls. Garnish with chopped walnuts, if desired.

Enjoy:
Serve warm or chilled, and enjoy this heart-healthy apple cinnamon rice pudding as a comforting dessert or wholesome breakfast option.

Nutritional Information (Per Serving):

Calories: 250 kcal
Total Fat: 4g
Saturated Fat: 0.5g
Cholesterol: 0mg
Sodium: 160mg

Total Carbohydrates: 51g
Dietary Fiber: 5g
Total Sugars: 18g
Protein: 4g

Light cakes and cookies

Almond Flour Blueberry Muffins

Yield: 12 muffins
Preparation time: 15 minutes
Cooking time: 25 minutes

Ingredients:

- 2 cups (200g) almond flour
- 1/4 cup (30g) coconut flour
- 1 teaspoon baking powder
- 1/4 teaspoon baking soda
- 1/4 teaspoon salt
- 3 large eggs
- 1/4 cup (60ml) unsweetened applesauce
- 1/4 cup (60ml) maple syrup or honey
- 1/4 cup (60ml) almond milk (or any milk of choice)
- 1 teaspoon vanilla extract
- 1 cup (150g) fresh blueberries (or frozen, thawed)

Instructions:
Preheat the Oven:

Preheat your oven to 350°F (175°C). Line a muffin tin with paper liners or grease the cups with cooking spray.

Mix Dry Ingredients:
In a large mixing bowl, whisk together the almond flour, coconut flour, baking powder, baking soda, and salt until well combined.

Prepare Wet Ingredients:
In another bowl, beat the eggs lightly. Add the applesauce, maple syrup (or honey), almond milk, and vanilla extract. Mix until smooth.

Combine Wet and Dry:
Pour the wet ingredients into the bowl with the dry ingredients. Stir until just combined. Be careful not to overmix.

Fold in Blueberries:

Gently fold in the blueberries until evenly distributed throughout the batter.

Fill Muffin Cups:
Divide the batter evenly among the muffin cups, filling each about 3/4 full.

Bake:
Bake in the preheated oven for 22-25 minutes, or until the muffins are golden brown on top and a toothpick inserted into the center comes out clean.

Cool and Serve:
Allow the muffins to cool in the pan for 5 minutes, then transfer them to a wire rack to cool completely.

Enjoy:
Serve these heart-healthy almond flour blueberry muffins as a nutritious breakfast or snack option that's rich in fiber and antioxidants.

Nutritional Information (Per Serving - 1 muffin):

Calories: 160 kcal
Total Fat: 10g
Saturated Fat: 1g
Cholesterol: 47mg
Sodium: 125mg

Total Carbohydrates: 13g
Dietary Fiber: 3g
Total Sugars: 7g
Protein: 6g

Greek Yogurt with Honey and Nuts

Yield: 2 servings
Preparation time: 5 minutes

Ingredients:

- 300g Greek yogurt (unsweetened)
- 2 tablespoons (30ml) honey
- 30g mixed nuts (such as almonds, walnuts, and pecans)
- Fresh berries (optional, for garnish)

Instructions:

Prepare the Greek Yogurt:
Measure out the Greek yogurt and divide it equally into two serving bowls.

Drizzle with Honey:
Drizzle 1 tablespoon of honey over each bowl of Greek yogurt, evenly distributing it over the surface.

Add Nuts:
Roughly chop the mixed nuts and sprinkle them over the Greek yogurt and honey mixture.

Optional Garnish:
If desired, garnish each bowl with a few fresh berries, such as strawberries or blueberries, for extra flavor and antioxidants.

Serve:
Serve immediately as a heart-healthy breakfast or snack option.

Nutritional Information (Per Serving):

Calories: 250 kcal
Total Fat: 12g
Saturated Fat: 1.5g
Cholesterol: 10mg
Sodium: 45mg

Total Carbohydrates: 25g
Dietary Fiber: 2g
Total Sugars: 21g
Protein: 14g

Oatmeal Raisin Cookies

Yield: 12 cookies
Preparation time: 15 minutes
Cooking time: 12-15 minutes

Ingredients:

- 100g rolled oats
- 60g whole wheat flour
- 1 teaspoon ground cinnamon
- 1/2 teaspoon baking powder
- 1/4 teaspoon salt

- 60ml unsweetened applesauce
- 60ml maple syrup
- 1 tablespoon (15ml) olive oil
- 1 teaspoon vanilla extract
- 40g raisins

Instructions:

Preheat the Oven:
Preheat your oven to 180°C (350°F) and line a baking sheet with parchment paper.

Prepare the Dry Ingredients:
In a mixing bowl, combine the rolled oats, whole wheat flour, ground cinnamon, baking powder, and salt. Mix well.

Combine Wet Ingredients:
In another bowl, whisk together the unsweetened applesauce, maple syrup, olive oil, and vanilla extract until well combined.

Combine Wet and Dry Ingredients:
Pour the wet ingredients into the bowl of dry ingredients and mix until everything is evenly incorporated. Fold in the raisins.

Form Cookie Dough:
Using a spoon or cookie scoop, portion out the dough and place it onto the prepared baking sheet, spacing the cookies apart to allow for spreading.

Flatten the Cookies:
Use the back of a spoon or your fingers to gently flatten each cookie to your desired thickness.

Bake the Cookies:
Place the baking sheet in the preheated oven and bake for 12-15 minutes, or until the cookies are golden brown around the edges.

Cool and Serve:
Allow the cookies to cool on the baking sheet for a few minutes before transferring them to a wire rack to cool completely.

Nutritional Information (Per Serving – 1 cookie):

Calories: 90 kcal
Total Fat: 2g
Saturated Fat: 0.3g
Cholesterol: 0mg
Sodium: 50mg

Total Carbohydrates: 16g
Dietary Fiber: 2g
Total Sugars: 6g
Protein: 2g

Peanut Butter Banana Bites

Yield: 12 bites
Preparation time: 10 minutes
Chilling time: 30 minutes

Ingredients:

- 2 medium bananas
- 60g natural peanut butter
- 30g rolled oats

- 15g unsweetened shredded coconut
- 15g dark chocolate chips (optional)
- 1/2 teaspoon ground cinnamon

- 1 tablespoon (15ml) honey or maple syrup (optional)

Instructions:
Prepare the Bananas:
Peel the bananas and cut them into 1-inch thick slices. Lay the slices flat on a parchment-lined baking sheet.
Spread Peanut Butter:
Spread a thin layer of peanut butter onto half of the banana slices. If the peanut butter is too thick, you can warm it slightly to make it easier to spread.
Prepare the Filling:
In a small bowl, combine the rolled oats, shredded coconut, dark chocolate chips (if using), ground cinnamon, and honey or maple syrup (if using). Mix well to combine.
Assemble the Bites:

- Chopped nuts or seeds for coating (optional)

Sprinkle the oat mixture over the peanut butter-covered banana slices. Top each with a plain banana slice to create sandwiches.
Optional Coating:
Roll each banana bite in chopped nuts or seeds for an extra crunch and nutrition boost.
Chill:
Place the assembled banana bites in the refrigerator and chill for at least 30 minutes to allow them to set.
Serve:
Once chilled, remove the banana bites from the refrigerator and serve. Enjoy immediately as a nutritious snack or dessert.

Nutritional Information (Per Serving - 1 bite):

Calories: 60 kcal
Total Fat: 3g
Saturated Fat: 1g
Cholesterol: 0mg
Sodium: 10mg

Total Carbohydrates: 8g
Dietary Fiber: 1g
Total Sugars: 4g
Protein: 1.5g

Whole Wheat Carrot Cake

Yield: 12 servings
Preparation time: 20 minutes
Cooking time: 30 minutes

Ingredients:

- 200g whole wheat flour
- 100g grated carrots
- 100ml unsweetened applesauce
- 100ml low-fat plain yogurt
- 80ml honey or maple syrup
- 60ml olive oil
- 2 eggs
- 1 teaspoon baking powder

- 1/2 teaspoon baking soda
- 1 teaspoon ground cinnamon
- 1/4 teaspoon ground nutmeg
- 1/4 teaspoon ground ginger
- 1/4 teaspoon salt
- 50g chopped walnuts (optional)
- 50g raisins (optional)

Instructions:
Preheat the Oven:
Preheat your oven to 180°C (350°F). Grease and flour a 9-inch round cake pan or line it with parchment paper.
Prepare the Dry Ingredients:
In a large mixing bowl, combine the whole wheat flour, baking powder, baking soda, ground cinnamon, ground nutmeg, ground ginger, and salt. Mix well to combine.
Prepare the Wet Ingredients:
In another bowl, whisk together the grated carrots, unsweetened applesauce, low-fat plain yogurt, honey or maple syrup, olive oil, and eggs until well combined.

Combine Wet and Dry Ingredients:
Gradually add the wet ingredients to the dry ingredients, stirring until just combined. Be careful not to overmix.
Add Optional Ingredients:
Fold in the chopped walnuts and raisins if using, until evenly distributed throughout the batter.
Bake the Cake:
Pour the batter into the prepared cake pan and spread it out evenly. Bake in the preheated oven for 25-30 minutes, or until a toothpick inserted into the center comes out clean.

Cool and Serve:
Allow the cake to cool in the pan for 10 minutes, then transfer it to a wire rack to cool completely.

Optional Frosting:
If desired, you can top the cake with a light cream cheese frosting or a dusting of powdered sugar before serving.

Nutritional Information (Per Serving):

Calories: 180 kcal
Total Fat: 7g
Saturated Fat: 1g
Cholesterol: 30mg
Sodium: 150mg

Total Carbohydrates: 27g
Dietary Fiber: 3g
Total Sugars: 11g
Protein: 4g

Coconut and Date Energy Balls

Yield: 12 energy balls
Preparation time: 15 minutes

Ingredients:

- 100g pitted dates
- 50g rolled oats
- 50g unsweetened shredded coconut
- 30g almond butter
- 15ml honey or maple syrup

- 10g chia seeds
- 5g flaxseed meal
- 5ml vanilla extract
- Pinch of salt

Instructions:
Prepare the Dates:
If the dates are not soft, soak them in warm water for 10 minutes to soften. Drain well before using.
Combine Ingredients:
In a food processor, combine the pitted dates, rolled oats, unsweetened shredded coconut, almond butter, honey or maple syrup, chia seeds, flaxseed meal, vanilla extract, and a pinch of salt.
Process Until Smooth:
Process the mixture in the food processor until it forms a sticky dough-like consistency. Stop and scrape down the sides of the bowl as needed to ensure all ingredients are well incorporated.

Form into Balls:
Once the mixture is evenly combined, use clean hands to roll it into 12 evenly sized balls. If the mixture is too sticky, wet your hands slightly to prevent sticking.
Chill and Serve:
Place the energy balls on a baking sheet lined with parchment paper and chill them in the refrigerator for at least 30 minutes to firm up.
Store or Serve:
Once chilled, the energy balls can be stored in an airtight container in the refrigerator for up to two weeks. Enjoy them as a quick and nutritious snack whenever you need a boost of energy!

Nutritional Information (Per Serving - 1 Energy Ball):

Calories: 80 kcal
Total Fat: 4g
Saturated Fat: 1.5g
Cholesterol: 0mg
Sodium: 10mg

Total Carbohydrates: 10g
Dietary Fiber: 2g
Total Sugars: 6g
Protein: 2g

Mixed Berry Crumble

Yield: 6 servings
Preparation time: 15 minutes
Cooking time: 30 minutes

Ingredients:

- **For the Filling:**
- 400g mixed berries (such as strawberries, blueberries, raspberries, and blackberries)
- 30g granulated sugar (or sweetener of choice)
- 15ml lemon juice
- 5g cornstarch (optional, for thickening)
- **For the Crumble Topping:**
- 50g rolled oats

- 40g almond flour
- 30g chopped almonds
- 20g unsweetened shredded coconut
- 30ml maple syrup or honey
- 30ml coconut oil, melted
- 5g ground cinnamon
- Pinch of salt

Instructions:
Preheat the Oven:
Preheat your oven to 180°C (350°F). Lightly grease a baking dish with coconut oil or non-stick cooking spray.
Prepare the Berry Filling:
In a mixing bowl, combine the mixed berries, granulated sugar (or sweetener), lemon juice, and cornstarch (if using). Toss until the berries are evenly coated. Transfer the berry mixture to the prepared baking dish and spread it out evenly.
Make the Crumble Topping:
In another mixing bowl, combine the rolled oats, almond flour, chopped almonds, unsweetened shredded coconut, maple syrup or honey, melted coconut oil, ground

cinnamon, and a pinch of salt. Mix until the ingredients are well combined and the mixture is crumbly.
Assemble and Bake:
Sprinkle the crumble topping evenly over the berry filling in the baking dish.
Bake:
Place the baking dish in the preheated oven and bake for 25-30 minutes, or until the berry filling is bubbling, and the crumble topping is golden brown and crisp.
Serve Warm:
Once baked, remove the mixed berry crumble from the oven and let it cool for a few minutes before serving. Enjoy warm on its own or with a dollop of Greek yogurt or a scoop of vanilla frozen yogurt.

Nutritional Information (Per Serving):

Calories: 200 kcal
Total Fat: 10g
Saturated Fat: 4g
Cholesterol: 0mg
Sodium: 50mg

Total Carbohydrates: 25g
Dietary Fiber: 5g
Total Sugars: 15g
Protein: 4g

Chocolate and Avocado Brownies

Yield: 12 servings
Preparation time: 15 minutes
Cooking time: 25 minutes

Ingredients:

- 200g ripe avocado (about 1 large avocado)
- 100g dark chocolate (at least 70% cocoa), chopped
- 75g unsweetened applesauce
- 100g honey or maple syrup
- 2 large eggs
- 5ml vanilla extract

- 50g unsweetened cocoa powder
- 50g almond flour
- 5g baking powder
- Pinch of salt
- Optional toppings: chopped nuts, dark chocolate chips

Instructions:

Preheat the Oven:
Preheat your oven to 180°C (350°F). Grease a square baking pan (about 8x8 inches) with coconut oil or line it with parchment paper.

Prepare the Avocado:
Cut the avocado in half, remove the pit, and scoop out the flesh into a food processor or blender.

Melt the Chocolate:
In a microwave-safe bowl, melt the dark chocolate in 30-second intervals, stirring in between until smooth. Alternatively, you can melt the chocolate using a double boiler on the stove.

Blend the Avocado:
Add the ripe avocado to the food processor or blender and blend until smooth.

Mix Wet Ingredients:
In a mixing bowl, combine the blended avocado, melted dark chocolate, unsweetened applesauce, honey or maple syrup, eggs, and vanilla extract. Mix until well combined.

Combine Dry Ingredients:
In another mixing bowl, sift together the cocoa powder, almond flour, baking powder, and a pinch of salt.

Combine Wet and Dry Ingredients:
Gradually add the dry ingredients to the wet ingredients, stirring until just combined. Be careful not to overmix.

Bake:
Pour the brownie batter into the prepared baking pan and spread it out evenly. If desired, sprinkle chopped nuts or dark chocolate chips on top.
Bake in the preheated oven for 25-30 minutes, or until the edges are set, and a toothpick inserted into the center comes out with a few moist crumbs.

Cool and Serve:
Allow the brownies to cool in the pan for about 10 minutes before slicing into squares. Serve warm or at room temperature.

Nutritional Information (Per Serving):

Calories: 150 kcal
Total Fat: 9g
Saturated Fat: 3g
Cholesterol: 30mg
Sodium: 50mg

Total Carbohydrates: 16g
Dietary Fiber: 3g
Total Sugars: 10g
Protein: 4g

Pumpkin Spice Energy Bars

Yield: 12 bars
Preparation time: 15 minutes
Cooking time: 25 minutes

Ingredients:

- 200g canned pumpkin puree
- 100g almond butter
- 80ml maple syrup
- 1 teaspoon vanilla extract
- 150g rolled oats
- 40g almond flour
- 30g ground flaxseed

- 1 teaspoon ground cinnamon
- 1/2 teaspoon ground ginger
- 1/4 teaspoon ground nutmeg
- 1/4 teaspoon ground cloves
- 40g chopped nuts (such as walnuts or pecans)
- 40g dried cranberries or raisins
- Pinch of salt

Instructions:

Preheat the Oven:
Preheat your oven to 180°C (350°F). Line a baking dish (about 8x8 inches) with parchment paper, leaving some overhang for easy removal.

Mix Wet Ingredients:

In a mixing bowl, combine the canned pumpkin puree, almond butter, maple syrup, and vanilla extract. Mix until smooth and well combined.

Add Dry Ingredients:
Add the rolled oats, almond flour, ground flaxseed, ground cinnamon, ground ginger, ground nutmeg, ground cloves, chopped nuts, dried cranberries or raisins,

and a pinch of salt to the bowl. Stir until all ingredients are evenly incorporated.

Press Into Baking Dish:

Transfer the mixture to the prepared baking dish. Use a spatula or your hands to press the mixture evenly into the dish, ensuring it's tightly packed.

Bake:

Bake in the preheated oven for 25-30 minutes, or until the edges are golden brown and the bars are set.

Cool and Slice:

Remove the baking dish from the oven and let it cool completely on a wire rack. Once cooled, lift the parchment paper to remove the bars from the dish and transfer them to a cutting board. Use a sharp knife to slice the bars into squares or rectangles.

Store and Enjoy:

Store the pumpkin spice energy bars in an airtight container at room temperature for up to 1 week, or in the refrigerator for longer freshness. Enjoy as a nutritious snack or a quick energy boost on the go!

Nutritional Information (Per Serving):

Calories: 180 kcal
Total Fat: 9g
Saturated Fat: 1g
Cholesterol: 0mg
Sodium: 40mg

Total Carbohydrates: 20g
Dietary Fiber: 4g
Total Sugars: 9g
Protein: 5g

Banana Oat Cookies

Yield: 12 cookies
Preparation time: 10 minutes
Cooking time: 15 minutes

Ingredients:

- 2 ripe bananas (about 200g), mashed
- 120g rolled oats
- 30g almond flour
- 30g chopped walnuts or pecans
- 30g dried cranberries or raisins

- 1 tablespoon maple syrup
- 1 teaspoon ground cinnamon
- 1/2 teaspoon vanilla extract
- Pinch of salt

Instructions:

Preheat the Oven:

Preheat your oven to 180°C (350°F). Line a baking sheet with parchment paper.

Mix Wet Ingredients:

In a large mixing bowl, combine the mashed bananas, maple syrup, vanilla extract, and ground cinnamon. Mix well until smooth.

Add Dry Ingredients:

Add the rolled oats, almond flour, chopped nuts, dried cranberries or raisins, and a pinch of salt to the bowl with the wet ingredients. Stir until everything is well combined and forms a thick cookie dough.

Form Cookies:

Using a spoon or your hands, scoop out about 1 1/2 tablespoons of the cookie dough and shape it into a

cookie. Place it onto the prepared baking sheet. Repeat with the remaining dough, spacing the cookies about 2 inches apart.

Bake:

Transfer the baking sheet to the preheated oven and bake for 15-18 minutes, or until the cookies are golden brown and set.

Cool and Enjoy:

Once baked, remove the cookies from the oven and let them cool on the baking sheet for 5 minutes. Then, transfer them to a wire rack to cool completely. Enjoy these heart-healthy banana oat cookies as a nutritious snack or dessert option!

Nutritional Information (Per Serving - 1 Cookie):

Calories: 80 kcal
Total Fat: 2.5g

Saturated Fat: 0.3g
Cholesterol: 0mg

Sodium: 10mg
Total Carbohydrates: 13g
Dietary Fiber: 2g

Total Sugars: 5g
Protein: 2g

Almond Butter Chocolate Chip Cookies

Yield: 12 cookies
Preparation time: 10 minutes
Cooking time: 12-15 minutes

Ingredients:

- 120g almond butter (unsweetened)
- 60g almond flour
- 60g rolled oats
- 60ml maple syrup
- 1 egg

- 1 teaspoon vanilla extract
- 30g dark chocolate chips (at least 70% cocoa)
- 1/2 teaspoon baking soda
- Pinch of salt

Instructions:
Preheat the Oven:
Preheat your oven to 180°C (350°F). Line a baking sheet with parchment paper.
Mix Wet Ingredients:
In a large mixing bowl, combine the almond butter, maple syrup, egg, and vanilla extract. Mix well until smooth and creamy.
Add Dry Ingredients:
Add the almond flour, rolled oats, baking soda, and a pinch of salt to the bowl with the wet ingredients. Stir until everything is well combined and forms a thick cookie dough.
Fold in Chocolate Chips:
Gently fold in the dark chocolate chips until evenly distributed throughout the cookie dough.
Form Cookies:

Using a spoon or your hands, scoop out about 1 1/2 tablespoons of the cookie dough and shape it into a cookie. Place it onto the prepared baking sheet. Repeat with the remaining dough, spacing the cookies about 2 inches apart.
Bake:
Transfer the baking sheet to the preheated oven and bake for 12-15 minutes, or until the cookies are golden brown around the edges.
Cool and Enjoy:
Once baked, remove the cookies from the oven and let them cool on the baking sheet for 5 minutes. Then, transfer them to a wire rack to cool completely. Enjoy these heart-healthy almond butter chocolate chip cookies as a nutritious snack or dessert option!

Nutritional Information (Per Serving - 1 Cookie):

Calories: 150 kcal
Total Fat: 10g
Saturated Fat: 1g
Cholesterol: 16mg
Sodium: 63mg

Total Carbohydrates: 13g
Dietary Fiber: 2g
Total Sugars: 6g
Protein: 4g

Guilt-Free Indulgences

Indulging in your favorite treats doesn't have to derail your heart-healthy diet. By creating healthier versions of your go-to desserts, you can enjoy delicious flavors without the guilt. Opt for nutrient-rich ingredients like whole grains, nuts, seeds, and natural sweeteners. For instance, replace refined flour with almond or oat flour, and use dark chocolate instead of milk chocolate. Swap butter for heart-healthy fats like avocado or olive oil. Incorporate fruits and vegetables, such as adding pureed carrots or zucchini to muffins and cakes for added moisture and nutrients.

Portion control tips:

Portion control is essential in enjoying treats without overindulging. Here are some tips to help you maintain balance:

1. **Mindful Eating**: Savor each bite, focusing on the flavors and textures. Eating slowly can help you feel satisfied with smaller portions.
2. **Pre-Portion Treats**: Divide snacks into individual servings to avoid mindless overeating.
3. **Use Smaller Plates**: This visual trick can make portions appear larger, helping you feel satisfied with less.
4. **Pair Treats with Healthy Foods**: Balance indulgences with nutrient-dense foods like fruits, vegetables, or a handful of nuts.
5. **Set Limits**: Decide in advance how much you'll eat and stick to it. This can prevent the temptation to go back for seconds.

By making smart ingredient choices and practicing portion control, you can enjoy guilt-free indulgences while maintaining a heart-healthy lifestyle.

Expert Tips for Optimal Health

Achieving and maintaining optimal health requires a holistic approach that includes balanced nutrition, regular physical activity, and effective stress management techniques. Here are some expert tips to guide you on your journey to a healthier lifestyle.

Nutrition Tips for Heart Health

Importance of Balanced Nutrition A balanced diet is crucial for heart health. Consuming a variety of nutrient-dense foods provides the vitamins, minerals, and antioxidants your body needs to function optimally. Prioritize whole foods such as fruits, vegetables, whole grains, lean proteins, and healthy fats.

Tips for Reducing Sodium and Fat Intake

1. **Read Labels**: Check food labels for sodium content and opt for low-sodium versions of your favorite products.
2. **Cook at Home**: Preparing meals at home allows you to control the amount of salt and fat in your food.
3. **Use Herbs and Spices**: Enhance flavor with herbs, spices, and citrus instead of salt.
4. **Choose Healthy Fats**: Replace saturated and trans fats with healthier options like olive oil, avocado, nuts, and seeds.
5. **Limit Processed Foods**: Processed and fast foods often contain high levels of sodium and unhealthy fats.

Exercise and Lifestyle Recommendations

Benefits of Regular Physical Activity Engaging in regular physical activity is essential for maintaining heart health. Exercise helps lower blood pressure, improve cholesterol levels, and boost overall cardiovascular fitness. Aim for at least 150 minutes of moderate-intensity aerobic exercise per week, such as brisk walking, cycling, or swimming.

Stress Management Techniques Managing stress is vital for overall well-being. Chronic stress can negatively impact heart health, leading to high blood pressure and increased risk of heart disease. Here are some effective stress management techniques:

1. **Meditation**: Practicing meditation can help calm the mind and reduce stress. Set aside a few minutes each day to sit quietly and focus on your breath or a calming mantra.
2. **Breathing Practices**: Deep breathing exercises can quickly reduce stress levels. Try techniques such as diaphragmatic breathing, where you inhale deeply through your nose, allowing your abdomen to expand, and exhale slowly through your mouth.
3. **Walks in Nature**: Spending time outdoors, especially in green spaces, can significantly reduce stress. Aim for a daily walk in a park or natural setting to clear your mind and rejuvenate your spirit.
4. **Peaceful Hobbies**: Engage in activities that bring you joy and relaxation, such as reading, gardening, or listening to music.
5. **Mindfulness**: Practice mindfulness by staying present in the moment and being aware of your thoughts and feelings without judgment. This can help you manage stress more effectively.

3. Maintaining Long-Term Wellness

Building Healthy Habits Consistency is key to long-term wellness. Establishing healthy habits that become part of your daily routine can lead to lasting benefits. Start with small, manageable changes and gradually build on them. For example, begin by adding more fruits and vegetables to your diet, then incorporate regular exercise into your schedule.

Monitoring and Tracking Progress Keeping track of your progress can help you stay motivated and identify areas for improvement. Use a journal or digital app to record your meals, exercise, and stress management practices. Regularly review your entries to see how far you've come and to set new goals.

In conclusion, achieving optimal health requires a balanced approach that includes proper nutrition, regular physical activity, and effective stress management. By making conscious choices and building healthy habits, you can support your heart health and overall well-being for the long term. Remember, small changes can lead to significant improvements, so start today and enjoy the journey to a healthier you.

The Bonus Conscious 30-Day Meal Plan

Goals and Benefits of the Meal Plan

The Conscious 30-Day Meal Plan is designed to help you achieve optimal heart health by incorporating nutrient-dense, low-sodium, and low-saturated fat foods into your diet. This meal plan aims to:

- **Improve cardiovascular health:** By focusing on ingredients known to support heart health, this plan helps reduce the risk of heart disease and high blood pressure.
- **Promote weight management:** Balanced meals with controlled portion sizes help you maintain a healthy weight.
- **Enhance overall well-being:** Nutrient-rich foods improve energy levels, mood, and overall physical health.
- **Establish healthy eating habits:** Following this plan can help you develop sustainable, long-term healthy eating habits.

How to Follow the Plan

To get the most out of the Conscious 30-Day Meal Plan:

- **Follow the meal planners:** Stick to the suggested meals and snacks for each day.
- **Prepare in advance:** Use the weekly meal planners and shopping lists to stay organized and reduce daily meal preparation time.
- **Stay hydrated:** Drink plenty of water throughout the day.
- **Listen to your body:** Adjust portion sizes based on your hunger and energy needs.
- **Incorporate physical activity:** Combine the meal plan with regular exercise for optimal health benefits.

Week 1 Meal Planner

Day 1:

- Breakfast: Berry Banana Smoothie
- Snack: Apple Slices with Almond Butter
- Lunch: Quinoa and Black Bean Salad
- Snack: Greek Yogurt with Honey and Nuts
- Dinner: Lemon Herb Grilled Salmon

Day 2:

- Breakfast: Apple Cinnamon Overnight Oats
- Snack: Fresh Fruit Kabobs with Yogurt Dip
- Lunch: Mediterranean Hummus and Veggie Wrap
- Snack: Roasted Chickpeas with Spices
- Dinner: Vegetable Stir-Fry with Tofu

Day 3:

- Breakfast: Spinach and Mushroom Omelette
- Snack: Mixed Nuts and Dried Fruit Mix
- Lunch: Lentil Soup with Kale and Carrots
- Snack: Caprese Salad Skewers
- Dinner: Grilled Shrimp and Asparagus Skewers

Day 4:

- Breakfast: Greek Yogurt Parfait with Berries and Honey
- Snack: Spicy Edamame Beans
- Lunch: Tomato Basil and Mozzarella Sandwich
- Snack: Kale Chips with Sea Salt
- Dinner: Balsamic Glazed Pork Tenderloin

Day 5:

- Breakfast: Avocado Toast with Poached Egg
- Snack: Dark Chocolate Covered Strawberries
- Lunch: Asian-Inspired Chicken Salad
- Snack: Fresh Fruit Salad with Mint
- Dinner: Sweet Potato and Black Bean Enchiladas

Day 6:

- Breakfast: Quinoa Breakfast Bowl with Fresh Fruit
- Snack: Mini Quinoa and Spin

ach Patties

- Lunch: Chickpea and Spinach Curry
- Snack: Greek Yogurt and Berry Popsicles
- Dinner: Herb-Crusted Cod with Lemon

Day 7:

- Breakfast: Veggie-Packed Breakfast Burrito
- Snack: Cherry Tomato and Mozzarella Bites
- Lunch: Red Lentil and Carrot Soup
- Snack: Whole Wheat Pita Chips and Guacamole
- Dinner: Moroccan-Spiced Chicken Thighs

Week 1 Shopping List

- Fresh Produce: Bananas, berries, apples, spinach, mushrooms, avocados, quinoa, black beans, kale, carrots, cherry tomatoes, mozzarella, lemons, asparagus, sweet potatoes, bell peppers, zucchini
- Proteins: Greek yogurt, salmon, tofu, shrimp, chicken breast, cod, chicken thighs
- Grains and Legumes: Whole wheat bread, whole wheat pita, lentils

Snacks and Extras: Almond butter, mixed nuts, dried fruit, dark chocolate, edamame, chickpeas, hummus

Week 2 Meal Planner

Day 8:

- Breakfast: Almond Butter and Banana Whole Wheat Pancakes
- Snack: Cucumber and Avocado Sushi Rolls
- Lunch: Shrimp and Avocado Salad
- Snack: Carrot and Zucchini Muffins
- Dinner: Roasted Vegetable and Quinoa Salad

Day 9:

- Breakfast: Steel-Cut Oats with Nuts and Dried Fruit
- Snack: Roasted Red Pepper and Walnut Dip
- Lunch: Barley and Vegetable Stir-Fry
- Snack: Broccoli and Cheddar Bites
- Dinner: Grilled Chicken and Avocado Wrap

Day 10:

- Breakfast: Blueberry Chia Seed Pudding
- Snack: Avocado Deviled Eggs
- Lunch: Curried Chickpea Salad
- Snack: Fresh Fruit Kabobs with Yogurt Dip
- Dinner: Quinoa Stuffed Bell Peppers

Day 11:

- Breakfast: Sweet Potato and Black Bean Hash
- Snack: Spicy Black Bean Dip with Veggie Sticks
- Lunch: Greek Salad with Lemon Vinaigrette
- Snack: Coconut and Date Energy Balls
- Dinner: Teriyaki Tofu and Broccoli Stir-Fry

Day 12:

- Breakfast: Heart-Healthy Granola with Almond Milk
- Snack: Spicy Edamame Beans
- Lunch: Turkey and Veggie Lettuce Wraps
- Snack: Dark Chocolate Covered Strawberries
- Dinner: Vegan Butternut Squash Risotto

Day 13:

- Breakfast: Egg White and Veggie Frittata
- Snack: Mixed Nuts and Dried Fruit Mix
- Lunch: Mediterranean Hummus and Veggie Wrap
- Snack: Caprese Salad Skewers
- Dinner: Baked Chicken with Garlic and Rosemary

Day 14:

- Breakfast: Whole Grain Waffles with Fresh Berries
- Snack: Cherry Tomato and Mozzarella Bites
- Lunch: Red Lentil and Carrot Soup
- Snack: Kale Chips with Sea Salt
- Dinner: Moroccan-Spiced Chicken Thighs

Week 2 Shopping List

- Fresh Produce: Bananas, berries, apples, spinach, mushrooms, avocados, quinoa, black beans, kale, carrots, cherry tomatoes, mozzarella, lemons, asparagus, sweet potatoes, bell peppers, zucchini, red peppers, butternut squash
- Proteins: Greek yogurt, salmon, tofu, shrimp, chicken breast, cod, chicken thighs
- Grains and Legumes: Whole wheat bread, whole wheat pita, lentils
- Snacks and Extras: Almond butter, mixed nuts, dried fruit, dark chocolate, edamame, chickpeas, hummus, coconut, dates

Daily Meal Plan Breakdown

Breakfast, Lunch, Dinner, and Snack Suggestions

- **Breakfast:** Start your day with a nutrient-rich meal such as a smoothie, oatmeal, or a veggie-packed omelette.
- **Lunch:** Opt for salads, wraps, and soups that are filling and packed with heart-healthy ingredients.
- **Dinner:** Focus on lean proteins, whole grains, and a variety of vegetables for a balanced meal.
- **Snacks:** Choose healthy snacks like fresh fruit, nuts, yogurt, and vegetable sticks with hummus.

Tips for Meal Prep and Cooking Ahead

- **Plan Ahead:** Use the weekly meal planners and shopping lists to prepare for the week.
- **Batch Cooking:** Prepare large portions of grains, proteins, and vegetables to use throughout the week.
- **Healthy Snacking:** Keep healthy snacks readily available to avoid unhealthy choices.
- **Stay Organized:** Label and store prepped meals and ingredients for easy access.

By following the Conscious 30-Day Meal Plan, you can enjoy delicious, heart-healthy meals that support your overall well-being. With careful planning and preparation, maintaining a nutritious diet becomes simple and sustainable.

Encouragement and Final Tips:

Congratulations, dear Readers, on your remarkable achievement of completing your journey through the Heart Healthy Cookbook for Beginners. By embracing these heart-healthy recipes, you've not only enhanced your well-being and vitality but also demonstrated your commitment to a heart-healthy lifestyle.
Remember, a healthy heart is not just about what you eat but also about the lifestyle choices you make every day.
As you continue your path to heart health, here are some crucial final tips that will continue to support and guide you:
Stay Consistent: Incorporate these heart-healthy recipes into your daily meals. Consistency is critical to reaping long-term benefits.
Stay Active: Combine a balanced diet with regular physical activity. Aim for at least 30 minutes of moderate exercise most days of the week.
Monitor Your Health: Regularly check your blood pressure, cholesterol levels, and weight. Consult healthcare professionals for personalized guidance.
Enjoy in Moderation: While these recipes are designed to be heart-healthy, moderation is essential. This means enjoying treats occasionally, such as a small piece of dark chocolate or a single scoop of ice cream and balancing them with nutrient-dense meals
Stay Informed: Keep educating yourself about heart health. Knowledge empowers you to make informed decisions.

Remember, every small step towards a healthier lifestyle is a significant contribution to your well-being. Your dedication to a heart-healthy diet is not just an investment in yourself but also in the health and happiness of your loved ones.

Wishing you continued success and good health on your journey!

Sincerely yours, Abilene Higss

Appendices

Glossary of Heart-Healthy Terms

Antioxidants: Compounds that protect cells from damage caused by free radicals. Found in fruits, vegetables, nuts, and seeds.

Cholesterol: A fatty substance produced by the liver and obtained from certain foods. High levels can increase the risk of heart disease.

Fiber: A type of carbohydrate found in plant foods that aids digestion, promotes satiety, and helps lower cholesterol levels.

Omega-3 Fatty Acids: Essential fats that are beneficial for heart health, found in fatty fish (salmon, mackerel), flaxseeds, chia seeds, and walnuts.

Polyunsaturated Fats: Healthy fats that help lower LDL cholesterol levels when consumed in moderation. Found in nuts, seeds, and vegetable oils like soybean and sunflower oil.

Monounsaturated Fats: Healthy fats that can help improve blood cholesterol levels and decrease the risk of heart disease. Found in olive oil, avocados, and nuts.

Soluble Fiber: Fiber that dissolves in water and helps lower cholesterol levels. Found in oats, barley, fruits (apples, oranges), and vegetables (carrots, broccoli).

Whole Grains: Grains that include the entire grain kernel (bran, germ, endosperm). Examples include whole wheat, oats, quinoa, and brown rice.

Plant Sterols and Stanols: Compounds found in plants that can help lower cholesterol levels. They are added to some margarines, orange juice, and yogurt.

Lean Protein: Protein sources that are low in saturated fats. Examples include lean cuts of poultry, fish, legumes, and tofu.

Sodium: A mineral found in salt that, when consumed in excess, can raise blood pressure and increase the risk of heart disease.

Trans Fats: Unhealthy fats that are formed during the process of hydrogenation and found in partially hydrogenated oils. They raise LDL cholesterol levels and increase the risk of heart disease.

Superfoods: Nutrient-dense foods that provide health benefits beyond their basic nutritional content. Examples include berries, spinach, salmon, and nuts.

Portion Control: Managing the amount of food consumed in a meal or snack to ensure balanced nutrition and healthy weight management.

Hydration: Maintaining adequate water intake, which is essential for overall health and heart function.

Low-Glycemic Index Foods: Foods that raise blood sugar levels slowly, which can help manage weight and reduce the risk of heart disease. Examples include whole grains, legumes, and non-starchy vegetables.

Phytonutrients: Natural compounds found in plants that have antioxidant and anti-inflammatory properties, promoting heart health.

Probiotics: Beneficial bacteria that promote gut health and may have indirect benefits for heart health by improving digestion and immune function.

Prebiotics: Types of fiber that promote the growth of beneficial bacteria in the gut, supporting overall health and potentially heart health.

Conversion Charts

Volume Conversions:

- 1 teaspoon (tsp) = 5 milliliters (ml)
- 1 tablespoon (tbsp) = 15 milliliters (ml)
- 1 fluid ounce (fl oz) = 30 milliliters (ml)
- 1 cup = 240 milliliters (ml)
- 1 pint (pt) = 480 milliliters (ml)
- 1 quart (qt) = 0.95 liters (l)
- 1 gallon (gal) = 3.8 liters (l)

Weight Conversions:

- 1 ounce (oz) = 28 grams (g)
- 1 pound (lb) = 16 ounces (oz) = 454 grams (g)

Dry Ingredient Conversions:

- 1 cup all-purpose flour = 120 grams (g)
- 1 cup granulated sugar = 200 grams (g)
- 1 cup brown sugar = 200 grams (g)
- 1 cup powdered sugar = 120 grams (g)
- 1 cup rolled oats = 90 grams (g)
- 1 cup nuts (whole) = 150 grams (g)
- 1 cup butter = 225 grams (g)

Temperature Conversions:

- 350°F = 180°C
- 375°F = 190°C
- 400°F = 200°C
- 425°F = 220°C

Oven Temperature Conversions:

- Slow oven = 275°F = 140°C
- Moderate oven = 350°F = 180°C
- Hot oven = 425°F = 220°C

Liquid Conversions:

- 1 liter (l) = 1,000 milliliters (ml)
- 1 liter (l) ≈ 4.2 cups

Metric to Imperial Conversions:

- 1 centimeter (cm) = 0.39 inches

- 1 meter (m) = 39.37 inches = 3.28 feet
- 1 kilogram (kg) = 2.2 pounds (lb)
- 1 milliliter (ml) = 0.034 fluid ounces (fl oz)
- 1 liter (l) = 1.06 quarts (qt)
- 1 kilometer (km) = 0.62 miles

Resources and References

1. **Books:**
   - "The Prevent and Reverse Heart Disease Cookbook" by Ann Crile Esselstyn and Jane Esselstyn
   - "The Mediterranean Diet Weight Loss Solution" by Julene Stassou MS RD
   - "The Blue Zones Solution" by Dan Buettner
2. **Scientific Articles and Journals:**
   - American Heart Association journals such as Circulation and Journal of the American Heart Association
   - British Medical Journal (BMJ) - Heart
   - Journal of the American College of Cardiology (JACC)
3. **Websites and Online Resources:**
   - Mayo Clinic - Heart-Healthy Diet: https://www.mayoclinic.org/healthy-lifestyle/nutrition-and-healthy-eating/in-depth/mediterranean-diet/art-20047801
   - American Heart Association - Healthy Eating: https://www.heart.org/en/healthy-living
   - Harvard Health - Heart Health: https://www.health.harvard.edu/topics/heart-health
4. **Government Health Organizations:**
   - National Institutes of Health (NIH) - Heart, Lung, and Blood Institute: https://www.nhlbi.nih.gov/health-topics/heart-healthy-living
   - Centers for Disease Control and Prevention (CDC) - Heart Disease: https://www.cdc.gov/heartdisease/index.htm
5. **Academic Research Papers:**
   - PubMed - National Library of Medicine: https://pubmed.ncbi.nlm.nih.gov/
   - Google Scholar: https://scholar.google.com/

Recipe Index

Dried Fruit

    Mixed Nuts and Dried Fruit Mix, 63

    Steel-Cut Oats with Nuts and Dried Fruit, 28

Edamame

    Edamame and Quinoa Salad, 36

    Edamame Hummus, 67

    Spicy Edamame Beans, 71

Egg

    Avocado Deviled Eggs, 70

    Avocado Toast with Poached Egg, 22

    Egg White and Veggie Frittata, 22

    Savory Oatmeal with Spinach and Parmesan, 27

    Spinach and Mushroom Omelette, 21

    Veggie-Packed Breakfast Burrito, 25

Egg Whites

    Egg White and Veggie Frittata, 22

Enchiladas

    Sweet Potato and Black Bean Enchiladas, 55

French Toast

    Baked Apple Cinnamon French Toast, 30

Fresh Fruit

    Fresh Fruit Kabobs with Yogurt Dip, 68

    Fresh Fruit Salad with Mint, 80

    Quinoa Breakfast Bowl with Fresh Fruit, 24

Fresh Fruit Kabobs

    Fresh Fruit Kabobs with Yogurt Dip, 68

Fresh Mint

    Fresh Fruit Salad with Mint, 80

Garlic

    Baked Chicken with Garlic and Rosemary,48

Greek Yogurt

    Greek Yogurt and Berry Popsicles, 68

    Greek Yogurt Parfait with Berries and Honey, 17

    Greek Yogurt with Honey and Nuts, 84

    Tuna Salad with Greek Yogurt Dressing, 37

Greek Yogurt Dressing

Cherry Tomato and Mozzarella Bites, 69

Tomato Basil and Mozzarella Sandwich, 42

Mushroom

Spinach and Mushroom Omelette, 21

Mushrooms

Stuffed Portobello Mushrooms, 57

Nuts

Greek Yogurt with Honey and Nuts, 84

Mixed Nuts and Dried Fruit Mix, 63

Steel-Cut Oats with Nuts and Dried Fruit, 28

Parmesan

Savory Oatmeal with Spinach and Parmesan, 27

Pasta

Whole Wheat Pasta Primavera, 43

Peach

Cottage Cheese and Peach Breakfast Bowl, 25

Peanut Butter

Peanut Butter Banana Bites, 85

Pesto

Zucchini Noodles with Pesto and Cherry Tomatoes, 43

Pineapple

Mango and Pineapple Smoothie Bowl, 18

Pineapple Coconut Smoothie, 82

Pita Chips

Whole Wheat Pita Chips and Guacamole, 66

Poppy Seed Dressing

Spinach and Strawberry Salad with Poppy Seed Dressing, 37

Pork

Balsamic Glazed Pork Tenderloin, 49

Portobello Mushrooms

Stuffed Portobello Mushrooms, 57

Pumpkin Spice

Pumpkin Spice Energy Bars, 89

Quinoa

Edamame and Quinoa Salad, 37

Mini Quinoa and Spinach Patties, 72

Mini Quinoa and Spinach Patties, 72

Strawberries

Berry Banana Smoothie, 16

Greek Yogurt Parfait with Berries and Honey, 17

Spinach and Strawberry Salad with Poppy Seed Dressing, 37

Sweet Potato

Baked Sweet Potato Fries, 71

Sweet Potato and Black Bean Chili, 40

Sweet Potato and Black Bean Enchiladas, 55

Sweet Potato and Black Bean Hash, 26

Teriyaki

Teriyaki Tofu and Broccoli Stir-Fry, 58

Tofu

Teriyaki Tofu and Broccoli Stir-Fry, 58

Vegetable Stir-Fry with Tofu, 52

Tomato

Cherry Tomato and Mozzarella Bites, 69

Spicy Black Bean Dip with Veggie Sticks, 66

Tomato and Avocado Breakfast Sandwich, 23

Tomato Basil and Mozzarella Sandwich, 42

Tomato Glaze

Turkey Meatloaf with Tomato Glaze, 59

Tuna

Tuna Salad with Greek Yogurt Dressing, 37

Turkey

Turkey and Veggie Lettuce Wraps, 45

Turkey Meatloaf with Tomato Glaze, 60

Veggies

Chickpea and Veggie Buddha Bowl, 33

Mediterranean Hummus and Veggie Wrap, 46

Spicy Black Bean Dip with Veggie Sticks, 65

Veggie-Packed Breakfast Burrito, 25

Vinaigrette

Greek Salad with Lemon Vinaigrette, 38

Walnuts

Roasted Red Pepper and Walnut Dip, 64

Whole Wheat Flour

Almond Butter and Banana Whole Wheat Pancakes, 27

Whole Grain Waffles with Fresh Berries, 29

Whole Wheat Carrot Cake, 86

Whole Wheat Pasta Primavera, 43

Whole Wheat Pita Chips and Guacamole, 66

Zucchini

Carrot and Zucchini Muffins, 73

Zucchini Noodles with Pesto and Cherry Tomatoes, 43

Disclaimer

The information provided in this cookbook, "Heart Healthy Cookbook for Beginners: 1800 Days of Simple, Low-Fat, Low-Sodium Recipes. Expert Tips for Complete Guide to Lifelong Wellness & Bonus," is for general informational purposes only. While the author, Abilene Higgs, has made every effort to ensure the accuracy of the information within this book, the content is provided "as is" without warranty of any kind, express or implied.
The recipes and nutritional information are intended for general guidance and should not replace the advice of a medical professional. Individuals with specific dietary needs or medical conditions should seek the advice of a qualified health care provider before starting any diet or exercise program. The author and publisher disclaim any liability in connection with the use of this information.

The author, Abilene Higgs, is not responsible for any adverse effects or consequences resulting from the use of any recipes, suggestions, or procedures described in this book. The reader assumes full responsibility for any risks, injuries, or damages resulting from the use of the information provided in this book.

All product names, trademarks, and registered trademarks are the property of their respective owners. Their use does not imply any affiliation with or endorsement by them.